GCSE
Eduqas Spanish
REVISION GUIDE
FOR THE GRADE 9–1 COURSE

Bethan McHugh and
Chris Whittaker

Crown House Publishing
www.crownhouse.co.uk

First published by
Crown House Publishing Ltd
Crown Buildings, Bancyfelin, Carmarthen, Wales, SA33 5ND, UK
www.crownhouse.co.uk
and
Crown House Publishing Company LLC
PO Box 2223
Williston, VT 05495, USA
www.crownhousepublishing.com

Cover images © Alfonso de Tomás, © dikobrazik, © robodread – Fotolia.com
Icons, pages 4–5, 9, 11, 13, 15, 17, 108–141, © schinsilord – Fotolia.
Page 7, © LuckyImages – Fotolia: Pages 18–19, © JB Fontana – Fotolia: Page 21, © Milkos – Fotolia:
Page 23, © micromonkey – Fotolia: Page 25, © julien tromeur – Fotolia: Page 27, © lassedesignen –
Fotolia: Pages 28–29, © Brian Jackson – Fotolia: Page 31, © BillionPhotos.com – Fotolia: Page 33, ©
Lsantilli – Fotolia: Page 34, © WaveBreakMediaMicro – Fotolia: Page 37, © Focus Pocus LTD – Fotolia:
Pages 38–39, © koss13 – Fotolia: Page 41, © exclusive-design – Fotolia: Page 43, © Tupungato – Fotolia:
Page 44, © luckyli – Fotolia: Page 45, © Mik Man – Fotolia: Pages 48–49, © Lukassek – Fotolia: Page
51, © Kara – Fotolia: Page 53, © silver-john – Fotolia: Page 55, © Aleksandar Todorovic – Fotolia: Page
57, © connel_design – Fotolia: Pages 58–59, © Black Spring – Fotolia: Page 63, © Premium Collection –
Fotolia: Page 67, © zhu difeng – Fotolia: Pages 68–69, © peshkov – Fotolia: Page 73, © icsnaps – Fotolia:
Page 74, © sanchos303 – Fotolia: Page 77, © monkeybusiness – Fotolia: Pages 78–79, © sebra – Fotolia:
Page 83, © Vladimir Melnikov – Fotolia: Page 85, © Antonio Gravante – Fotolia: Page 87, © Tom Wang
– Fotolia: Pages 88–89, © mikola249 – Fotolia: Page 91, © zhu difeng – Fotolia: Page 93, © pathdoc –
Fotolia: Page 95, © djile – Fotolia: Page 97, © goodluz – Fotolia: Pages 98–99, © Konstantin Yuganov
– Fotolia: Page 101, © connel_design – Fotolia: Page 103, © Syda Productions – Fotolia: Page 105,
© faithie – Fotolia: Page 107, © javiindy – Fotolia.

British Library of Cataloguing-in-Publication Data

A catalogue entry for this book is available from the British Library.

Print ISBN 978-178583272-7

Printed and bound in the UK by Pureprint Group, Uckfield, East Sussex

CONTENTS

INTRODUCING EDUQAS GCSE SPANISH

Your Eduqas Spanish GCSE is split into three main themes:

- IDENTITY AND CULTURE
- LOCAL, NATIONAL, INTERNATIONAL AND GLOBAL AREAS OF INTEREST
- CURRENT AND FUTURE STUDY AND EMPLOYMENT

Your four Spanish exams (SPEAKING, LISTENING, READING and WRITING) will cover these three themes equally. Each exam is worth 25% of your final grade. You are not allowed to use a dictionary in any exam.

Now for the confusing bit! Each of these three themes has three sub-themes which are divided into two sections each. These sections are all of equal importance – so don't spend all of your time concentrating on your favourites! Make sure you revise all the topics equally.

IDENTITY AND CULTURE	LOCAL, NATIONAL, INTERNATIONAL AND GLOBAL AREAS OF INTEREST	CURRENT AND FUTURE STUDY AND EMPLOYMENT
YOUTH CULTURE • Self and relationships • Technology and social media	**HOME AND LOCALITY** • Local areas of interest • Transport	**CURRENT STUDY** • School/college life • School/college studies
LIFESTYLE • Health and fitness • Entertainment and leisure	**SPAIN AND SPANISH-SPEAKING COUNTRIES** • Local and regional features and characteristics • Holidays and tourism	**WORLD OF WORK** • Work experience and part-time jobs • Skills and personal qualities
CUSTOMS AND TRADITIONS • Food and drink • Festivals and celebrations	**GLOBAL SUSTAINABILITY** • Environment • Social issues	**JOBS AND FUTURE PLANS** • Applying for work/study • Career plans

This revision guide covers all of the themes and sub-themes, as well as giving tips and advice on how to prepare for each exam with plenty of exam-style questions and grammar practice to help you. ¡Buena suerte!

SPEAKING EXAM

The first exam you will do is the speaking one. This is usually quite a bit earlier than the other three exams. The whole exam will last about 20 minutes, including your preparation time. This is what will happen:

1. You will go to a preparation room with an invigilator and you will be given a booklet. This booklet contains your role play and photo card. You will have 12 minutes to prepare for the exam and make notes. You can't write full sentences or a script but you should have time to think about what you are going to say and note some useful keywords and phrases.
2. Once your preparation time is up, you will go into the exam room with your teacher. You will take your notes with you. Once the teacher has recorded your name and candidate number, etc. the exam will begin. You will complete the role play, then the photo card and finally the conversation. The recording will not be stopped between each section.

ROLE PLAY

Your role play will look something like this:

Escenario: Estás hablando con tu amigo/a español/a sobre la salud. Tu profesor/a es el/la amigo/a y habla primero.

- El deporte (**dos** detalles)
- La comida rápida – opinión
- !
- ? salud
- La comida – ayer

There will be a sentence at the start in Spanish which is the escenario and explains the theme of the role play. Don't worry too much if you don't understand every word. The important bit here is the theme – la salud – and the second sentence, which tells you who will speak first (usually, but not always, your teacher).

There are **five** bullet points in every role play. Be careful because one of those bullet points will ask for **two** details. You will need to give **two** pieces of information to get the mark – e.g. Juego al tenis y al golf.

When you see **!** you will have to respond to a question you have not prepared for. In your preparation time, try to think of the sort of thing which you may be asked.

When you see **?** you will have to **ask** a question. This could be quite a simple question – e.g. ¿Haces deporte?

At Foundation level, **one** of the prompts will be in a different tense (usually the past). Watch out for clues like ayer (yesterday), el año pasado (last year), el fin de semana pasado (last weekend). At Higher level, there will be **two** prompts in a different tense. Look out for clues to use the future or conditional – e.g. mañana (tomorrow), la semana que viene (next week), en el futuro (in the future).

Unlike other parts of the speaking exam, you won't get any extra marks for adding in further details, opinions, etc. In the role play you only have to give the information asked for in the bullet points and nothing more.

You may have to give an opinion or point of view. It doesn't matter whether you really think this or not as long as you say something.

Try to answer in a complete sentence using an appropriate verb – e.g. la comida rápida es malsana not just malsana.

PHOTO CARD

You will have your photo and **two** questions in advance, so there is no excuse for not having full, extended answers ready. Your teacher doesn't want you to read a script, but you should have a good idea of what to say. Your card will look something like this:

- Describe la foto. (Foundation)/¿De qué trata esta foto? (Higher)
- ¿Prefieres celebrar tu cumpleaños con tus amigos o con tu familia? ¿Por qué? Do you prefer celebrating your birthday with your friends or with your family? Why?

The first question on the photo card will always ask you to describe the photo. There is no fixed amount you have to say but you should be aiming for at least **three** or **four** details for maximum marks – e.g. Who is in the photo? What are they doing? Where are they? Why are they there? What else is in the photo? What do you think about the photo?

The second question will usually ask for an opinion. Try to elaborate as much as you can. Make sure you justify and explain your opinions and give as much information as possible.

UNSEEN QUESTIONS

Your teacher will then ask you **two** unseen questions. In the first unseen question, you will usually have to comment on an opinion – e.g.:

- Creo que las fiestas de cumpleaños son caras. ¿Estás de acuerdo? I think birthday parties are expensive. Do you agree?

The last question will usually need to be answered in a different tense – e.g.:

- Describe tu último cumpleaños. Describe your last birthday.
- ¿Cómo sería tu cumpleaños ideal? What would your ideal birthday be like?

In your preparation time try to think of some of the things you might be asked in the unseen questions. Listen carefully to what the teacher says and don't guess – if you don't understand, ask your teacher to repeat the question. You won't lose any marks and this will buy you extra thinking time! You don't have to agree with the opinion given by the teacher.

Here are some useful phrases and questions:

Spanish	English
Describe ...	Describe …
¿Crees que ...?	Do you think that …?
¿Cuáles son los aspectos negativos/positivos de ...?	What are the negative/positive aspects of …?
¿Cuáles son las ventajas y desventajas de ...?	What are the advantages and disadvantages of …?
En tu opinión ...	In your opinion …
¿Estás de acuerdo?	Do you agree?
¿Por qué?	Why?
¿Prefieres ...?	Do you prefer …?
¿Qué tipo de ... te interesa/prefieres?	What type of … do you like/prefer?
¿Te gusta(n) ...?	Do you like …?
¿Te gustaría ...?	Would you like …?
Justifica/explica tu opinión	Justify/explain your opinion

CONVERSATION

The conversation lasts for 3–5 minutes (Foundation) or 5–7 minutes (Higher). This is split equally between two parts:

- Part 1 – You will have agreed this in advance with your teacher. You will start this part of the conversation by saying what you have chosen to talk about.
- Part 2 – This will be on a different theme.

The conversation is your chance to show off the full extent of your knowledge of the language. What you say doesn't have to be factually correct as long as your Spanish makes sense! You need to make sure that you are able to give some answers in the past, present and future tense to access the highest marks. Try to give additional details, opinions and justifications wherever possible and include some complex phrases.

What if I get stuck?

- If you don't understand a question, ask your teacher to repeat it.
- Don't worry if you can't remember a particular word, say something else instead.
- If you make a mistake, it's okay to correct yourself.

LISTENING EXAM

In the listening exam you can expect to hear different types of spoken language which may include monologues, conversations, discussions, interviews, announcements, adverts and messages.

- Before the exam starts, you will have 5 minutes reading time. Don't waste this time filling in your name and candidate number! Use the time to read the questions carefully and make sure you know what you have to do etc. Make a note of any keywords and phrases which may be useful.
- Read the questions and make sure you are giving the required information – e.g. what, why, when, etc. Pay attention to negatives. The question 'Which hobby does she like?' requires a very different answer to 'Which hobby does she **not** like?'
- The paper will usually start with the easier questions and get harder throughout.
- You will hear each extract twice.
- There are **nine** questions but they are not all worth the same amount of marks. There are some 4, 5 and 6 mark questions so make sure you pay attention to this!
- Check carefully how many marks are available for the question. If you are asked to tick four boxes, make sure you don't tick more than four. You will lose marks if you do.
- Read the question carefully and listen to the recording for any keywords related to the question. Check the question again to make sure you have a clear idea of what exactly is being asked. Listen to the recording for a second time. Finalise your answer.
- There will be **two** questions in Spanish on your paper. You won't know where they will be until you see your paper and they might not be next to each other. They will probably ask for an answer in the form of a tick or a letter, etc. but you might have to write something in Spanish. If you write in English you won't get the mark, even if it's right. Always answer in the same language as the question.
- Don't leave any answers blank. Make an educated guess!

READING EXAM

In the reading exam you can expect to see a range of texts of different lengths, written in formal and informal styles and for a variety of audiences – e.g. magazine articles, information leaflets, adverts, literary texts, etc.

- Like the listening exam, the reading paper will usually start with the easier questions and gradually get harder – but the translation into English will always be the last question.
- There will be **two** questions about literary texts. Don't worry too much about these and treat them the same as any other reading question.
- You will have **three** questions in Spanish which, as with the listening exam, could be anywhere on the paper. You won't know where they will be until you see your paper and they might not be next to each other. They will probably ask for an answer in the form of a tick or a letter, etc. but you might have to write something in Spanish. If you write in English you won't get the mark, even if it's right. Always answer in the same language as the question.
- Read the question carefully and scan through the text for any keywords related to the question. Check the question again to make sure you are clear exactly what is being asked.
- At Foundation level, all the questions are worth 6 marks but at Higher level there will be some harder 8 mark questions at the end of the paper.
- Don't leave any questions unanswered – try to rule out any options you are sure are wrong before making a sensible guess.
- For the translation, don't translate the text word for word – ensure your translation makes sense in the target language – and check you are correctly translating the tenses.
- Check carefully how many marks are available for the question. If you are asked to tick four boxes, make sure you don't tick more than four. You will lose marks for this.

The following is a guide to the types of rubrics and instructions that might be used in the listening and reading exams:

Spanish	English
Completa la frase/las frases	Complete the phrase/phrases
Contesta a las preguntas en español	Answer the questions in Spanish
Elige ...	Choose ...
Elige .... para cada persona	Choose ... for each person
Elige la respuesta correcta	Choose the correct answer
Empareja ...	Match ...
Escribe la letra correcta en la casilla	Write the correct letter in the box
Escribe la letra correcta en el espacio	Write the correct letter in the gap
Escucha el anuncio de radio/la entrevista ...	Listen to the radio announcement/interview ...

Lee la información/este anuncio/los comentarios	Read the information/this advert/the commentaries
Marca (✓) dos casillas para cada pregunta	Tick (✓) two boxes for each question
Marca (✓) la casilla correcta para cada pregunta	Tick (✓) the correct box for each question
Marca (✓) seis casillas	Tick (✓) six boxes
Rellena el formulario/la tabla en español	Complete the form/the table in Spanish
Rellena los espacios en español	Fill in the blanks in Spanish
Escribe el nombre/el numero correcto	Write the correct name/number

WRITING EXAM

In the writing exam, try to bear the following points in mind:

- Check how many marks are available for each question so you know how to divide your time.
- See how many words you are recommended to write.
- Make a plan before you start writing.
- Always leave time to check your work.

Make sure you have:

- Been consistent with spellings.
- Used the correct gender for nouns.
- Used tenses appropriately.
- Used the correct endings for verbs.
- Included a range of sentence structures and vocabulary.
- Used a range of opinions and justifications.

Foundation: This exam is split into four questions.
- Question 1 – You will have to write six short sentences in Spanish about the headings provided. Keep it short and simple!
- Question 2 – You will have to write approximately 60 words in total about the three bullet points provided. Try to write an equal amount for each bullet point and make sure you include opinions.
- Question 3 – You will have to write 90–120 words in total about the three bullet points provided. You will be expected to use different tenses in this question.
- Question 4: Translation – You will have to translate five sentences into Spanish.

Higher: This exam is split into three questions.
- Question 1 – You will have to write 90–120 words in total about the three bullet points provided. You will be expected to use different tenses in this question.
- Question 2 – You will have to write 150–180 words. There is a choice of two titles (**don't** write a response for both!). You will be expected to justify your ideas and points of view and use a range of tenses.
- Question 3: Translation – You will have to translate a paragraph into Spanish.

Here are the sorts of rubrics and instructions that might be used in the writing exam. These examples are all in the **tú** form but you might get some instructions in the **usted** form if the examiners want you to write a piece of more formal Spanish – e.g. a job application letter.

Spanish	English
Elige …	Choose …
Escribe aproximadamente 60 palabras en español	Write approximately 60 words in Spanish
Escribe aproximadamente 90–120 palabras en español	Write approximately 90–120 words in Spanish
Escribe aproximadamente 150–180 palabras en español	Write approximately 150–180 words in Spanish
Escribe un artículo/un blog/una carta	Write an article/blog/letter
Presenta y justifica tus ideas y opiniones sobre uno de los temas siguientes	Present and justify your ideas and opinions on one of the following topics
Puedes dar más información, pero tienes que describir	You can give additional information but you must describe
Puedes dar más información, pero tienes que incluir	You can give additional information but you must include
Rellena el formulario en español	Complete the form in Spanish
Tienes que escribir una frase completa en cada espacio	You must write a complete sentence in each space
Escribe una frase completa sobre …	Write a complete sentence about …

THE BASICS

NUMBERS

CARDINAL NUMBERS

Start by learning numbers 0–30:

0	cero	8	ocho	16	dieciséis	24	veinticuatro
1	uno	9	nueve	17	diecisiete	25	veinticinco
2	dos	10	diez	18	dieciocho	26	veintiséis
3	tres	11	once	19	diecinueve	27	veintisiete
4	cuatro	12	doce	20	veinte	28	veintiocho
5	cinco	13	trece	21	veintiuno	29	veintinueve
6	seis	14	catorce	22	veintidós	30	treinta
7	siete	15	quince	23	veintitrés		

Next, make sure that you can count in tens up to 100:

10 diez
20 veinte
30 treinta
40 cuarenta
50 cincuenta
60 sesenta
70 setenta
80 ochenta
90 noventa
100 cien

Then make sure that you can fill in the gaps between 31 and 100. The same pattern continues all the way to 100:

31	treinta y uno	38	treinta y ocho
32	treinta y dos	39	treinta y nueve
33	treinta y tres	40	cuarenta
34	treinta y cuatro	41	cuarenta y uno
35	treinta y cinco	42	cuarenta y dos
36	treinta y seis	43	cuarenta y tres etc.
37	treinta y siete		

Cien is 100 but for the numbers 101–199 you use ciento:

101 ciento uno
102 ciento dos
103 ciento tres etc.

To get to 1000, all of the rules you have learned so far continue to apply. All you need to do now is learn to count in hundreds all the way to 1000:

100	cien
200	doscientos
300	trescientos
400	cuatrocientos
500	quinientos
600	seiscientos
700	setecientos
800	ochocientos
900	novecientos
1000	mil

Beyond 1000, all the same rules apply:

2000	dos mil
3000	tres mil
4000	cuatro mil etc.

ORDINAL NUMBERS (FIRST, SECOND, THIRD, ETC.)

primero	first
segundo	second
tercero	third
cuarto	fourth
quinto	fifth
sexto	sixth
séptimo	seventh
octavo	eighth
noveno	ninth
décimo	tenth

Ordinal numbers usually go before the noun and work like adjectives. In other words, they need to agree with the nouns they are describing – e.g. la **segunda** hora (the **second** hour), mis **primeros** días (my **first** days).

DATES

DAYS OF THE WEEK
Days of the week don't need a capital letter in Spanish.

lunes	Monday
martes	Tuesday
miércoles	Wednesday
jueves	Thursday
viernes	Friday
sábado	Saturday
domingo	Sunday

MONTHS

Like the days of the week, the months don't need a capital letter either.

enero	January
febrero	February
marzo	March
abril	April
mayo	May
junio	June
julio	July
agosto	August
septiembre	September
octubre	October
noviembre	November
diciembre	December

To express 'in a certain month' use the preposition **en** – e.g. voy a Francia **en** agosto (I'm going to France in August).

SEASONS

la primavera	spring
el verano	summer
el otoño	autumn
el invierno	winter

DATES

• Use normal numbers for dates – e.g. el seis de junio (the sixth of June), el treinta y uno de agosto (the thirty-first of August).
• Use el primero for the first of the month – e.g. **el primero** de enero (the first of January).

TIME

The verb **ser** is used to express the time of day. Use **es** when referring to one o'clock and use **son** when referring to all other hours:

Es la una.	It's one o'clock.
Son las dos.	It's two o'clock.
Son las tres.	It's three o'clock.
Son las cuatro.	It's four o'clock.

Minutes can be added to the hour using the word y (and):

Es la una **y** cinco.	It's five minutes past one.
Son las tres **y** doce.	It's twelve minutes past three.
Son las once **y** veinte.	It's twenty past eleven.

Minutes can be taken away from the hour (e.g. ten to, five to) using the word **menos** (less):

Es la una **menos** diez.	It's ten minutes to one.
Son las tres **menos** veinticinco.	It's twenty-five minutes to three.

You use **y media** (half past), **y cuarto** (quarter past) and **menos cuarto** (quarter to):

Es la una **y media**.	It's half past one.
Son las diez **y cuarto**.	It's quarter past ten.
Son las tres **menos cuarto**.	It's quarter to three.

To say something happens at a specific time, use **a la(s) + time** – e.g. las clases empiezan **a las nueve** (lessons start at nine o'clock).

ASKING QUESTIONS

Asking questions in Spanish is easy. You can turn statements into questions by adding question marks. This works in any tense – e.g.:

¿Vamos a salir?	Are we going to go out?
¿Fuiste al teatro?	Did you go to the theatre?
¿Irás a la playa?	Will you go to the beach?

Or you can use a question word – remember that they need accents.

¿Cómo?	How?
¿Qué?	What?
¿Quién? ¿Quiénes?	Who?
¿Dónde?	Where?
¿Cuál? ¿Cuáles?	Which?
¿Cuándo?	When?
¿Por qué?	Why?
¿Adónde?	Where (to)?
¿Cuánto?	How much?

IDENTITY AND CULTURE

YOUTH CULTURE

The sub-theme of **Youth Culture** is divided into two areas. Here are some suggestions of topics to revise:

SELF AND RELATIONSHIPS

- family relationships
- friendships
- physical appearance and self-image
- fashion and trends
- celebrity culture
- problems and pressures of young people
- marriage

TECHNOLOGY AND SOCIAL MEDIA

- different types of technology – e.g. tablets, mobiles, smart watches
- advantages and disadvantages of technology
- advantages and disadvantages of social media – e.g. cyberbullying
- impact of social media
- computer games
- future of technology
- how you use technology

TRANSLATION TIPS

ENGLISH TO SPANISH

- Don't translate sentences word for word!
- Check you are correctly translating the tense required.

SPANISH TO ENGLISH

- Don't translate the text word for word – you don't need to have the same number of words in your translation as the original text has.
- Don't miss out little but important words – e.g. very, often, never.
- Make sure you translate the correct meaning of the tense – e.g. I play, I played, I will play, I would play. Sometimes keywords and phrases – like yesterday, in the future, later, usually – will help you to identify the tense.

SELF AND RELATIONSHIPS

Describe a tu familia.
Describe your family.

Tengo una hermana que se llama Sophie. Me llevo bien con ella porque nos gusta la misma música. Es graciosa y nunca me molesta. También tengo un hermano mayor pero vive con su novia. Creo que mis padres son demasiado estrictos y preferiría tener más libertad.
I have a sister called Sophie. I get on well with her because we like the same music. She is fun and she never annoys me. I also have an older brother but he lives with his girlfriend. I think that my parents are too strict and I would prefer to have more freedom.

¿Qué hiciste con tus amigos el fin de semana pasado?
What did you do with your friends last weekend?

El viernes pasado fui al cine con mis compañeros de clase. Después de ver la película fuimos a un restaurante italiano y comimos pizza. Lo pasé muy bien.
Last Friday I went to the cinema with my school friends. After watching the film we went to an Italian restaurant and we ate pizza. I had a very good time.

¿Te importa la moda?
Is fashion important to you?

Claro que sí. Me inspiran los modelos y las celebridades y me encanta comprar ropa. En el futuro me gustaría trabajar en la industria de moda.
Yes of course. I'm inspired by models and celebrities and I love buying clothes. In the future I'd like to work in the fashion industry.

¿Admiras a alguna celebridad? ¿Por qué?
Is there a celebrity who you admire? Why?

Admiro a Ed Sheeran porque canta bien y tiene mucho talento. El año pasado asistí a su concierto. Fue increíble.
I admire Ed Sheeran because he sings well and is very talented. Last year I went to his concert. It was incredible.

¿Cómo sería tu novio/novia ideal?
What would your ideal boyfriend/girlfriend be like?

Tendría un buen trabajo y sería rico/a y generoso/a. En mi opinión, lo más importante es que tenga buen sentido del humor.
He/she would have a good job and be rich and generous. In my opinion, the most important thing is that he/she has a good sense of humour.

Try to use a variety of vocabulary and structures.
There's no need (and you won't have enough time) to describe the colour of every member of your family's hair, eyes, etc. The vocabulary you will be using could become really repetitive.

It's easy for this topic to become too descriptive and rely mainly on present tense. Try to include some opinions – what do you think of different family members? How do you get on? Why?

Say what you did/are going to do with your family to show off your use of different tenses.

GRAMMAR

Remember that both ser and estar mean 'to be' but in different ways.
- Ser is used with: physical description, personality and character, nationality, race, gender, professions, what things are made of, dates, days, seasons, time and possessions – e.g. **soy** alto/a (I am tall).
- Estar is used with: feelings, moods, emotions, physical conditions or appearances, marital status and location of things and people – e.g. **estoy** cansado/a (I am tired).
- You will have to use both **ser** and **estar** a lot in this sub-theme – make sure you use the correct one!

EXAM TASK

Translate the sentences into English:

1. Mi tía es trabajadora, deportista y muy inteligente.
2. Cuando era más joven, tenía muchos amigos.
3. Desgraciadamente, mi mejor amigo no se lleva muy bien con sus padres.
4. ¿Cuáles son las cualidades personales más importantes de un buen amigo?

Have you translated all the information? Does the sentence you have written make sense in English?

SELF AND RELATIONSHIPS

Admito que no me interesa la moda.	I have to admit that I am not interested in fashion.
Prefiero llevar ropa de diseño.	I prefer wearing designer clothes.
La vida de las celebridades me fascina.	I am fascinated by celebrities' lives.
Me gusta seguir la moda, pero adaptándola a mi propio estilo.	I like following fashion, but adapting it to my own style.
Me parece que la moda es demasiado cara.	As far as I am concerned, fashion is too expensive.
En mi opinión, tener una familia es muy importante.	In my opinion, having a family is very important.
Mi novio/novia ideal sería/haría/tendría …	My ideal girlfriend/boyfriend would be/would do/would have …
Discutimos a menudo.	We argue often.
Mi relación con mi hermanastro es tensa.	My relationship with my stepbrother is tense.
Nos entendemos perfectamente.	We understand each other perfectly.
No somos muy unidos.	We are not very close.
Me dejan hacer todo lo que quiero.	They let me do everything I want.
Me llevo fatal con mis hermanos.	I don't get on well with my siblings.
Mi madre me da consejos.	My mum gives me advice.
Tenemos los mismos gustos/intereses.	We have the same likes/interests.
Podemos hablar de todo.	We can talk about anything.
Mis padres siempre se meten en mis asuntos.	My parents always meddle in my business.
No me dejan salir.	They don't let me go out.
Raramente me critican.	They rarely criticise me.
Tengo suerte porque puedo confiar en mis amigos.	I am lucky because I can trust my friends.
Me cuesta resistirme a la presión de grupo.	I find it hard to resist peer pressure.
No quiero ser diferente.	I don't want to be different.
Me parezco a mi hermana.	I look like my sister.
Los jóvenes de hoy tienen muchos problemas.	Young people today have lots of problems.
La sociedad está obsesionada con las celebridades.	Society is obsessed with celebrities.

Use and adapt expressions like these in your speaking and writing exams to access higher marks.

EXAM TASK

Describe la foto. (Foundation)/¿De qué trata esta foto? (Higher)

En esta foto hay un grupo de estudiantes. Están en el colegio y no llevan uniforme. Creo que están hablando sobre la chica que está sola. Pienso que sufre acoso escolar. Además está triste porque no tiene amigos.

In this photo there is a group of students. They are at school and they are not wearing uniform. I think they are talking about the girl who is on her own. I think she is being bullied at school. What's more, she is sad because she doesn't have any friends.

Now can you answer these questions yourself?

- ¿Cómo son tus amigos? What are your friends like?
- Los amigos son más importantes que la familia. ¿Estás de acuerdo? Friends are more important than family. Do you agree?
- ¿Qué vas a hacer con tu familia el fin de semana que viene? What are you going to do with your family next weekend?

TECHNOLOGY AND SOCIAL MEDIA

¿Cuál es tu sitio web preferido y por qué?
What's your favourite website and why?

Prefiero Google porque lo utilizo para mis deberes y mi trabajo escolar. Es muy útil y se puede buscar cualquier cosa.
I prefer Google because I use it for my homework and my schoolwork. It's very useful and you can search for anything.

¿Te gustan las redes sociales? ¿Por qué (no)?
Do you like social media? Why (not)?

Me encanta utilizar las redes sociales para compartir mis ideas y chatear con mis amigos. También me gusta saber todo lo que pasa en el colegio.
I love using social media to share my ideas and chat with my friends. I also like knowing about everything that happens at school.

¿Cuáles son los aspectos negativos de la tecnología?
What are the negative aspects of technology?

La tecnología puede ser peligrosa porque en Internet no todo el mundo es quien dice ser. Hay que utilizar el sentido común y tener cuidado.
Technology can be dangerous because on the internet not everyone is who they say they are. You have to use common sense and take care.

¿Qué tipos de tecnología utilizaste ayer?
What types of technology did you use yesterday?

Leí un blog y mandé unos mensajes a mis amigos. Después de hacer mis deberes en el ordenador, descargué una película.
I read a blog and I sent some messages to my friends. After doing my homework on the computer, I downloaded a film.

¿Podrías vivir sin móvil?
Could you live without a mobile phone?

Para la mayoría de los jóvenes, un móvil es esencial.
Personalmente, no podría vivir sin mi móvil porque lo utilizo todo el tiempo para todo. ¡Creo que soy adicto/a!
For most young people, a mobile is essential. Personally, I couldn't live without my mobile because I use it all the time for everything. I think I'm addicted!

Hopefully you should have a lot to say about this topic!

You may be so in love with technology that you can't think of any disadvantages or problems, but it's important that you can offer a range of opinions. Learn a variety of ways of expressing your opinion – e.g. **pienso/ creo que** (I think/believe that), **me parece que** (it seems to me that), **en mi opinión** (in my opinion), **para mí** (for me), **a mi modo de ver** (as I see it), **(no) estoy de acuerdo** (I (don't) agree) – and try to use a range of adjectives. Examiners can get fed up of everything being **interesante** or **aburrido**.

EXAM TASK

Answer the questions in English.

Según algunos estudios, muchos jóvenes españoles (más de un 47 %) admiten ser adictos a las redes sociales hoy en día. La mayoría[1] de los jóvenes entre las edades de 15 y 19 años pasan hasta tres horas al día navegando las redes sociales y un 18 % de esos usuarios[2] no puede pasar más de una hora sin consultar sus cuentas[3]. Además, un 24 % comprueba[4] sus cuentas sociales antes de levantarse de la cama por las mañanas.

1 majority
2 users
3 accounts
4 check

1. What do many young people admit to being?
2. How much time do the majority of 15–19-year-olds spend on social media?
3. What percentage of young people check their accounts every hour?
4. What do 24% of young people do?
   (a) Check their accounts before they go to bed.
   (b) Check their accounts before they get up.
   (c) Check their accounts every night.

Watch out for distractors (annoying words the examiners put in to try to trick you) either in the questions or in the text! Be careful as there is more than one percentage mentioned in this text.

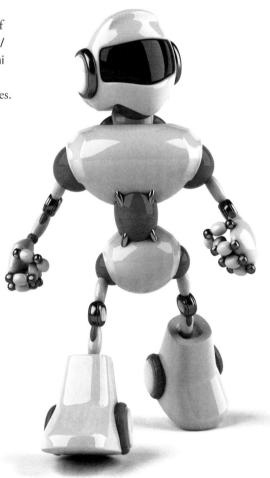

TECHNOLOGY AND SOCIAL MEDIA

Mis padres piensan que las redes sociales son una pérdida de tiempo.	My parents think that social media is a waste of time.
Tengo un portátil, pero está un poco anticuado.	I have a laptop but it's a bit old-fashioned.
Creo que la tecnología simplifica la vida diaria.	I think that technology simplifies everyday life.
Prefiero mi tablet porque es más fácil de utilizar.	I prefer my tablet because it's easier to use.
Utilizo mi móvil para sacar fotos y descargar música.	I use my mobile phone to take photos and download music.
No me gusta mi teléfono móvil porque es muy complicado.	I don't like my mobile phone because it's very complicated.
Me gusta hacer compras por Internet.	I like shopping online.
Ayer, navegué por Internet y usé mi ordenador para hacer mis deberes.	Yesterday I surfed the internet and I used my computer to do my homework.
Lo uso para todo.	I use it for everything.
Hay muchas ventajas y desventajas de la tecnología.	There are many advantages and disadvantages of technology.
Prefiero hablar con mis amigos cara a cara.	I prefer to talk to my friends face to face.
Me comunico siempre por las redes sociales.	I always communicate using social media.
Envío más mensajes que correos electrónicos.	I send more messages than e-mails.
My teléfono móvil tiene una cámara digital increíble.	My mobile phone has an incredible digital camera.
Tengo muchas canciones guardadas en mi portátil.	I have lots of songs saved on my laptop.
El ciberacoso me preocupa mucho.	Cyberbullying worries me a lot.
Nunca sabes con quien hablas por Internet.	You never know who you are talking to on the internet.
Mi abuela sabe mandar correos electrónicos.	My grandmother knows how to send e-mails.
La verdad es que soy adicto/a.	The truth is that I'm addicted.
Según mis padres, debería pasar menos tiempo en Internet.	According to my parents, I should spend less time on the internet.
Es importante hablar sobre los riesgos en línea.	It's important to talk about the risks online.

YOUTH CULTURE | 27

GRAMMAR

Negatives

Negative sentences are easy to form in Spanish – try to include some in your work.

To make a sentence negative, you usually put no before the verb – e.g. **no** tengo móvil (I don't have a mobile phone).

Another common negative word is nunca, which means never. It can go at the start of the sentence instead of no – e.g. **nunca** voy a comprar un ordenador (I'm never going to buy a computer). Or you can put no at the start and nunca at the end of the sentence – e.g. **no** voy a comprar un ordenador **nunca**.

Other common negative words that work in the same way as no and nunca are:

> nada – nothing
> nadie – no one
> ni ... ni – neither ... nor (e.g. no tengo **ni** móvil **ni** portátil)

Tienes que escribir una frase completa sobre:

EXAM TASK

- tu móvil
- los videojuegos
- las redes sociales
- la tecnología – opinión
- la música
- Internet – un problema

There's no need to write a really complicated sentence. A simple sentence can score full marks even if it has some minor errors. There isn't just one correct answer – e.g. for the first bullet point, you could say:

> Mi móvil es pequeño. My mobile phone is small.

Or you could even use a negative sentence:

> No tengo móvil. I haven't got a mobile phone.

IDENTITY AND CULTURE

LIFESTYLE

The sub-theme of **Lifestyle** is divided into two areas. Here are some suggestions of topics to revise:

HEALTH AND FITNESS

- healthy eating
- health issues – e.g. stress, illnesses
- unhealthy lifestyle – e.g. drugs, alcohol, smoking
- sports and exercise
- benefits of a healthy lifestyle

ENTERTAINMENT AND LEISURE

- music
- cinema
- television
- shopping
- eating out
- social activities and hobbies
- work–life balance

REMEMBER:

It's really important to keep revising questions – remember that you will have to answer unpredictable questions in your speaking exam and you will also have to ask a present tense question in the role play. You also have to talk about events in the past, present and future in the photo card discussion and conversation. It's really important that you are able to recognise questions in different tenses – e.g. ¿Qué haces normalmente? (What do you usually do?), ¿Qué hiciste la semana pasada? (What did you do last week?), ¿Qué harás la semana que viene? (What will you do next week?) Listen out for time phrases – e.g. mañana (tomorrow), ayer (yesterday), etc. – that will help you answer in the correct tense.

HEALTH AND FITNESS

¿Qué haces para mantenerte en forma?
What do you do to keep fit?

Hago muchas cosas para mantenerme en forma. Intento hacer deporte tres o cuatro veces a la semana y también como sano. Después de mis exámenes entrenaré todos los días.
I do lots of things to keep fit. I try to do sport three or four times a week and I also eat healthily. After my exams, I will train every day.

¿Prefieres jugar o ser espectador/a? ¿Por qué?
Do you prefer playing sport or being a spectator? Why?

Soy una persona muy deportista y soy miembro de varios equipos porque me encanta mantenerme activo/a. Sin embargo, me gusta mucho ver partidos de fútbol en el estadio porque el ambiente es fantástico.
I am a very sporty person and I am a member of several teams because I love being active. However, I really like watching football matches in the stadium because the atmosphere is fantastic.

¿Cuáles son los problemas de salud que te preocupan?
What are the health issues that worry you?

Me preocupan el tabaco y el alcohol. No se debe fumar porque puede causar enfermedades graves como el cáncer de pulmón. Beber alcohol es malo para la salud también. Muchos jóvenes se emborrachan regularmente, pero hay que beber con moderación.
I worry about tobacco and alcohol. You mustn't smoke because it can cause serious illnesses like lung cancer. Drinking alcohol is bad for your health as well. Many young people get drunk regularly, but you should drink in moderation.

¿Qué harás en el futuro para comer más sano?
What will you do in the future to eat more healthily?

Intentaré comer más fruta y me gustaría evitar la comida grasienta. Tengo la intención de tomar un buen desayuno todos los días y desgraciadamente tendré que comer menos chocolate.
I am going to try to eat more fruit and I would like to avoid fatty food. I intend to eat a good breakfast every day and unfortunately I will have to eat less chocolate.

¿Hiciste algún deporte el fin de semana pasado?
Did you do any sport last weekend?

El sábado por la mañana, hice footing con mi
hermano y luego fuimos al polideportivo para
hacer natación. ¡Estaba muy cansado/a!
Saturday morning, I went jogging with my
brother then we went to the sports centre to go
swimming. I was very tired!

GRAMMAR

Gustar and encantar

Remember that gustar and encantar don't work in
the same way as other verbs.

- Use gusta/encanta to describe single things or
  an activity (using a verb) – e.g. me **gusta** el
  deporte (I like sport), me **encanta** comer sano
  (I love eating healthily).
- Use gustan/encantan for two or more things –
  e.g. me **gustan** las verduras (I like vegetables),
  me **encantan** el tenis y el baloncesto (I love
  tennis and basketball).
- You need to use me, te, le, nos, os or les in
  front of the verb (these are called indirect object
  pronouns) – e.g. **le** gusta la fruta (he likes fruit),
  nos encantan los deportes acuáticos (we love
  water sports).
- Use mucho to say you like something a lot
  – e.g. me gusta **mucho** el chocolate (I like
  chocolate a lot).

Answer the questions in English.

EXAM TASK

Pásate por nuestro **gimnasio**: nuestros
entrenadores personales están para ayudarte
a alcanzar tu meta en el menor tiempo posible.
Diseñamos un plan de **acondicionamiento físico**
personalizado y adaptado a tus necesidades,
monitoreamos tu **alimentación** y te proponemos
un **plan nutricional**.

¡Aprovéchate ahora de nuestra oferta y consigue
el **entrenamiento personal** a un precio fantástico!
Sesión de 30 minutos por solo 17 € (o entrena
con otra persona por 30 € los dos) y sesión de 60
minutos por 22 €. Oferta especial para el mes de
febrero, bono de cinco sesiones solamente 65 €.
Visita nuestro sitio web o síguenos en las redes
sociales para más detalles.

1. What is the text about?
2. What will they do? Give **two** details.
3. What costs 30 euros?
4. Give **two** details about the special offer.
5. Where can you get more information? Give **one**
   detail.

**Question 1 is a new style of question which
you can expect to see in your listening and
reading exams.** Try to identify some keywords
(we have highlighted some in bold in this article
to help you – unfortunately that won't happen in
the real thing!). Make sure you read the whole text
before answering the question. Don't be distracted
by words that are not related to the overall theme
of the text – e.g. las redes sociales.

HEALTH AND FITNESS

Debería beber más agua.	I should drink more water.
He decidido que nunca voy a fumar.	I've decided that I am never going to smoke.
Voy a comer más fruta y verduras.	I am going to eat more fruit and vegetables.
Me gustaría comer menos caramelos.	I would like to eat fewer sweets.
Quisiera estar en forma.	I would like to be fit.
Si tuviera más dinero, compraría productos orgánicos.	If I had more money, I would buy organic products.
Necesito acostarme más temprano.	I need to go to bed earlier.
Cuando era más joven, comía demasiada comida rápida.	When I was younger, I ate too much fast food.
Se deberían comer cinco raciones de fruta y verduras al día.	You should eat five portions of fruit and vegetables a day.
Siempre tomo un buen desayuno.	I always eat a good breakfast.
Normalmente como bien, pero a veces como mal.	Normally I eat well, but sometimes I eat badly.
Es importante tener una dieta equilibrada.	It's important to have a balanced diet.
Como regularmente y nunca me salto ninguna comida.	I eat regularly and I never skip meals.
Los restaurantes de comida rápida se han hecho muy populares.	Fast-food restaurants have become very popular.
Todos sabemos que el ejercicio es importante porque ayuda a perder peso y reduce el riesgo de enfermedades.	We all know that exercise is important because it helps to lose weight and reduce the risk of illnesses.
Tengo muchas alergias e intolerancias alimentarias y tengo que evitar algunos tipos de comida.	I have many allergies and food intolerances and I have to avoid some types of food.
Iba al gimnasio todos los días, pero ahora prefiero hacer natación.	I used to go to the gym every day but now I prefer swimming.
Muchos jóvenes admiten haber probado las drogas.	Many young people admit to having tried drugs.
La mejor estrategia para que los niños coman de forma saludable es tener solo alimentos sanos en casa.	The best strategy to ensure children eat healthily is to only have healthy foods in the house.
Para mantenerse sano, se debe tener una dieta equilibrada.	To stay healthy, you must have a balanced diet.

Es fácil engancharse.	It's easy to get hooked.
La obesidad es un problema muy extendido.	Obesity is a very widespread problem.
Es esencial dormir bien.	It's essential to sleep well.
El estrés puede causar muchos problemas de salud.	Stress can cause many health problems.
Me preocupa mucho este problema.	I am very worried about this problem.
Se debe concienciar a los adolescentes de los peligros.	Young people must be made aware of the dangers.

You should aim to use connectives in extended sentences. Here are some useful examples to try to include in your speaking and writing:

antes (de) – before
después (de) – after
pero – but
porque – because
ya que – since
sin embargo – however
incluso – even
entonces – then
mientras – while/meanwhile
aunque – although
aún (si) – even (if)
también – also
además – what's more/furthermore

EXAM TASK

In the role play you will have to ask a question, use the present tense and at least one additional tense and respond to an unexpected question! Here are some examples of the prompts you might see:

- Tu salud (**dos** detalles)
- ? deporte
- La comida basura – opinión
- Una actividad – ayer
- ? cena
- La comida – la semana que viene

There are lots of different questions you could ask about sport.

You could keep it general – e.g. ¿Te gusta el deporte? (Do you like sport?) ¿Te gusta el fútbol? (Do you like football?)

Or be more specific – e.g. ¿Cuándo juegas al tenis? (When do you play tennis?) ¿Con quién juegas al baloncesto? (Who do you play basketball with?)

Watch out for 'trigger' words which mean your response needs to be in a different tense – e.g. ayer (yesterday), la semana que viene (next week).

ENTERTAINMENT AND LEISURE

¿Qué haces en tu tiempo libre?
What do you do in your free time?

Ahora mismo no tengo mucho tiempo libre a causa de mis exámenes, pero me encanta nadar. Voy a la piscina al menos tres veces a la semana. Como todo el mundo, veo la tele en casa y me gustan los videojuegos también.
At the moment I don't have much free time because of my exams, but I love swimming. I go to the swimming pool at least three times a week. Like everyone I watch TV at home and I like video games as well.

¿Crees que tener aficiones es importante para los jóvenes?
Do you think hobbies are important for young people?

Claro que sí. Hoy en día los jóvenes tienen muchos exámenes, entonces las aficiones son muy importantes porque ayudan a evitar el estrés.
Yes, of course. These days young people have lots of exams, so hobbies are really important because they help avoid stress.

¿Qué actividad te gustaría probar en el futuro?
What activity would you like to try in the future?

Me gustaría hacer esquí porque nunca lo he hecho y mi hermano me dijo que es increíble.
I'd like to go skiing because I've never done it and my brother told me it is incredible.

¿Qué hiciste el fin de semana pasado?
What did you do last weekend?

> No hice mucho porque tuve muchos deberes, pero fui a la casa de mi mejor amigo/a. Por la noche salimos juntos/as. Fue bastante divertido y lo pasé bien.
> I didn't do much because I had a lot of homework, but I went to my best friend's house. In the night we went out together. It was quite good fun and I had a good time.

¿Prefieres ir al cine o descargar una película? ¿Por qué?
Do you prefer going to the cinema or downloading a film? Why?

> Es muy caro ir al cine entonces prefiero descargar una película en casa. Además, mi salón es muchísimo más cómodo que el cine y puedo beber y comer lo que quiero.
> Going to the cinema is very expensive so I prefer downloading a film at home. What's more, my living room is much more comfortable than the cinema and I can eat and drink whatever I want.

Try to develop your answers as much as possible by adding extra detail wherever you can – e.g. to Voy al cine:

- Add who with – Voy al cine **con mis amigos**.
- Add a time phrase – Voy al cine con mis amigos **el viernes por la noche**.
- Add an opinion – Voy al cine con mis amigos el viernes por la noche. **Es divertido**.
- Add a justification – Voy al cine con mis amigos el viernes por la noche. Es divertido **porque el cine es muy grande**.
- Add a different tense – Voy al cine con mis amigos el viernes por la noche. Es divertido porque el cine es muy grande. **La semana pasada vimos una película de acción**.

EXAM TASK

Read the text then answer the questions below.
Lara: Yo estoy en contra de los videojuegos. A veces hay escenas de violencia y hay contenido no apto para los niños.

Arturo: Creo que algunos juegos tienen valor educativo. Por ejemplo, desarrollan los reflejos y mejoran la coordinación manual. Además, promueven el trabajo en equipo.

Raquel: Los niños pueden volverse adictos, prefiero salir con mis amigos que quedarme a jugar en casa.

Who do you think would say the following? Lara, Arturo or Raquel?

1. You can become addicted.
2. They are not suitable for children.
3. Some games are educational.
4. They promote teamwork.
5. I am against video games.
6. I would rather go out.

Be careful when answering Question 2 as both Lara and Raquel mention children!

ENTERTAINMENT AND LEISURE

Durante mi tiempo libre suelo ir de compras con mis amigos.	During my free time I usually go shopping with my friends.
Mis pasatiempos favoritos son la lectura y la fotografía.	My favourite hobbies are reading and photography.
Si tuviera más tiempo, aprendería a tocar un instrumento.	If I had more time, I would learn to play an instrument.
Toco la guitarra desde hace ocho años.	I've been playing the guitar for eight years.
Gasto demasiado dinero cuando salgo con mis amigos.	I spend too much money when I go out with my friends.
Cuando era pequeño solía jugar al baloncesto, pero ahora no me interesa.	When I was younger I used to play basketball, but now it doesn't interest me at all.
Me gusta leer cuando tengo un rato libre.	I like to read when I have a free moment.
Tengo que admitir que el tiempo libre es muy importante para mí.	I have to admit that free time is very important to me.
Me encantaba dibujar para relajarme, pero ahora prefiero ver la tele.	I used to love drawing to relax, but now I prefer watching TV.
En mi opinión, las actividades nos liberan de nuestra rutina diaria.	In my opinion, activities free us from our daily routine.
Creo que las aficiones nos permiten adquirir habilidades y conocimientos.	I think that hobbies allow us to acquire skills and knowledge.
Los hobbies o los pasatiempos son fundamentales para una buena salud física y mental.	Hobbies or pastimes are fundamental for good physical and mental health.
Me encanta escuchar todo tipo de música y podría pasar horas escuchando mis canciones favoritas.	I love listening to all types of music and I could spend hours listening to my favourite songs.
Es necesario encontrar el equilibrio entre los estudios y la vida personal.	It's necessary to find the balance between your studies and your personal life.
Tengo que decir que comprar cosas me da sensación de bienestar.	I have to say that buying things gives me a sense of well-being.
Es muy importante encontrar al menos dos horas semanales para realizar actividades físicas.	It's very important to find at least two hours a week for physical activities.

Me gustaría hacerme socio de un club.	I'd like to join a club.
Durante las vacaciones escolares tengo la intención de hacer más actividades al aire libre.	During the school holidays I intend to do more activities outside.
Mis padres piensan que los deberes son más importantes que el tiempo libre.	My parents think that homework is more important than free time.

GRAMMAR

Desde hace

You can use **desde hace** with the present tense to say how long you have been doing something – e.g. **juego al tenis desde hace** cinco meses (I've been playing tennis for five months).

GRAMMAR

Opinions in the past

It's really important to give opinions about things in the past as well as the present tense. The easiest way to do this is to use **era** (it was – imperfect tense) followed by an adjective – e.g. **era** fantástico (it was fantastic).

You can also use **fue** (it was – preterite tense) instead of **era** to give an opinion about a specific time or event in the past – e.g. la noche **fue** divertida (the night was fun). Remember to make the adjective agree with the noun if you are describing something feminine!

EXAM TASK

Translate these sentences into Spanish:

1. Last week I went shopping and I spent a lot of money.
2. Next weekend I am going to go to the cinema with my family.
3. What do you like doing in your free time?
4. I can't go out tomorrow because I have too much homework.

Remember:

- Don't translate word for word.
- Don't leave any gaps.
- Watch out for different tenses.
- Be careful with negatives.

IDENTITY AND CULTURE

CUSTOMS AND TRADITIONS

The sub-theme of **Customs and Traditions** is divided into two areas. Here are some suggestions of topics to revise:

FOOD AND DRINK
- party food and drink
- regional specialities
- eating habits
- cultural traditions
- food and drink for special occasions
- eating out

FESTIVALS AND CELEBRATIONS
- annual festivals and holidays
- birthdays
- national events
- regional events
- music festivals
- celebrating family occasions

REMEMBER:
- You need to use a variety of tenses in your written and spoken Spanish.
- Use your verb tables to help you when you are planning your work.
- Remember to use the correct verb ending – this tells the examiner who the sentence is about. You need to use the yo form to talk about yourself, but you need to learn other verb forms as well so that you can talk about other people.
- Try to include more detail by adding time expressions where possible – e.g. hoy (today), todos los días (every day), esta semana (this week), normalmente (usually), ayer por la noche (yesterday night), el fin de semana pasado (last weekend), hace dos meses (two months ago), mañana por la mañana (tomorrow morning), el año que viene (next year), etc.

FOOD AND DRINK

¿Te gusta cocinar? ¿Por qué (no)?
Do you like cooking? Why (not)?

> Cuando era más pequeño/a me gustaba hornear pasteles con mi madre. ¡Ahora solamente preparo bocadillos! Me encantan los programas de cocina, pero nunca tengo tiempo para cocinar.
> When I was younger, I liked baking cakes with my mother. Now I only make sandwiches! I love cookery programmes but I never have time to cook.

Describe tu última visita a un restaurante.
Describe your last visit to a restaurant.

> Fui a un restaurante italiano con mis padres el fin de semana pasado. Comí lasaña y de postre elegí un helado enorme. La cena fue deliciosa así que me gustaría volver al restaurante para mi cumpleaños.
> I went to an Italian restaurant with my parents last weekend. I ate lasagne and for dessert I chose a huge ice cream. The dinner was delicious so I'd like to go back to the restaurant for my birthday.

¿Crees que es importante probar la comida regional durante las vacaciones? ¿Por qué (no)?
Do you think it's important to try regional food on holiday? Why (not)?

> En mi opinión, los turistas deberían respetar la cultura de la zona. Creo que es esencial probar la comida local. Además, los restaurantes turísticos pueden ser muy caros.
> In my opinion, tourists should respect the culture of the region. I think it's essential to try local foods. What's more, tourist restaurants can be very expensive.

¿Cuál sería tu comida ideal?
What would your ideal meal be?

> Mi comida ideal sería en un restaurante en la playa en el Caribe. Probaría las especialidades locales y bebería cocteles tropicales.
> My ideal meal would be in a restaurant on the beach in the Caribbean. I would try local specialities and I would drink tropical cocktails.

¿Qué piensas de los platos preparados?
What do you think of ready meals?

Como los platos preparados de vez en cuando, por ejemplo, las pizzas congeladas, porque no me gusta cocinar. Pienso que los platos preparados son rápidos y prácticos, pero prefiero la comida casera.
I eat ready meals from time to time, for example frozen pizzas, because I don't like cooking. I think ready meals are quick and practical but I prefer home-cooked meals.

You may have to talk or write about the sort of food and drink you normally have at a celebration – e.g. a birthday party. Show the examiner that you're hungry for success by using different tenses and adding some intensifiers to improve your work.

GRAMMAR

Quantifiers and intensifiers
Try to add detail to your written and spoken Spanish by including quantifiers and intensifiers – e.g.:

bastante – enough
demasiado – too (much)
un poco – a little
mucho – a lot
muy – very

EXAM TASK

Read this literary text and answer the questions in English.

Daniel se acercó a curiosear unos libros que había a la entrada del restaurante. Era toda una estantería repleta de libros de cocina. Los títulos eran muy extraños: *Secretos de la cocina del mercado, Mil y una maneras de freír un pescado.*

No eran más que aburridos libros de cocina, un mundo que a Daniel no le interesaba. Ni la cocina ni la comida que salía de ella. Sin embargo, hubo un volumen que llamó su atención porque tenía unos bonitos dibujos. Se sentó en el sillón, junto a la ventana. Y, por primera vez en su vida, comenzó a leer un libro de recetas.

1. Where was the bookshelf?
2. What sort of books were they?
3. What was Daniel's opinion about these books in general?
4. Why did one particular book catch his attention?
5. What was remarkable about him starting to read it?

There will be two extracts from literary texts in your reading exam. Treat them just like any other reading comprehension task. Don't worry if you can't understand every single word.

FOOD AND DRINK

Cocinar es un talento que desgraciadamente no tengo.	Cooking is a talent that unfortunately I do not have.
Mi especialidad en la cocina es quemar las cosas.	My speciality in the kitchen is burning things.
No tengo tiempo para cocinar y suelo comprar platos preparados.	I don't have time to cook and I usually buy ready meals.
No me gustan los platos precocinados porque me resulta difícil identificar sus ingredientes.	I don't like ready meals because I find it hard to identify their ingredients.
Muchas personas piensan que abrir un envase y calentarlo en el microondas cuenta como cocinar.	Many people think that opening a carton and heating it in the microwave counts as cooking.
En los últimos años el hábito de comer en familia se ha visto disminuido.	In the last few years it has become less common to eat as a family.
Los platos preparados suelen contener porcentajes muy altos de grasa y sal.	Ready meals usually contain very high percentages of fat and salt.
La única cosa que hago bien son las tostadas de pan.	The only thing I'm good at making is toast.
Me gusta degustar la comida tradicional de los lugares que visito.	I like tasting traditional food from the places I visit.
Comer fuera de casa puede ser muy práctico y ahorra tiempo a veces.	Eating out can be very practical and sometimes saves time.
Las porciones que se sirven en los restaurantes son mayores de lo que requiere una persona típica.	The portions they serve in restaurants are bigger than what an average person needs.
Las comidas familiares dan a los niños la oportunidad de tener conversaciones con los adultos.	Family meals give children the opportunity to have conversations with adults.
Reunirse a comer en familia es un hábito que lleva a una mejor alimentación.	Getting together to eat as a family leads to better eating habits.
Las personas que no desayunan adecuadamente tienden a picar más entre horas.	People who don't eat a good breakfast tend to snack more in between meals.
Es bueno planificar las cenas de toda la semana para que sean variadas.	It's good to plan your evening meals for the week so that they are varied.
Cada fin de semana compramos comida india para llevar.	Every weekend we buy an Indian takeaway.
No soy muy fanática de la comida muy picante.	I'm not a big fan of spicy food.

No soporto las verduras ni la ensalada, pero sé que debería comerlas.	I can't stand vegetables or salad, but I know I should eat them.
Desde mi punto de vista hay demasiados programas dedicados a la cocina.	From my point of view there are too many cookery programmes.
Estamos rodeados de programas de cocina y muchos chefs se han vuelto celebridades.	We are surrounded by cookery programmes and many chefs have become celebrities.
Una de las cosas que más me gusta de viajar es disfrutar de la gastronomía y cultura de una región.	One of the things I like the most about travelling is enjoying the cuisine and culture of a region.
Si tuviera la oportunidad de viajar, me encantaría probar comidas exóticas.	If I had the opportunity to travel, I would love to try exotic food.
Me encanta probar cosas nuevas.	I love trying new things.

GRAMMAR

Adverbs of place and time

You will need to recognise and use the following adverbs:

hoy – today
mañana – tomorrow
ayer – yesterday
ahora – now
ya – already
a veces – sometimes
a menudo – often
siempre – always
aquí – here
allí – there

EXAM TASK

Escribe un artículo para un blog. Tienes que incluir:

- tu última visita a un restaurante
- lo que comiste y bebiste
- tus opiniones

Escribe aproximadamente 90–120 palabras en español.

Remember:
- Try to stick closely to the recommended word count in the exam.
- There is nothing to be gained by writing more than the recommended word count – in fact, your work may become less accurate and you may run out of time for other questions.
- Divide your time equally between all three bullet points.
- Draft a brief plan before you start writing.
- Leave enough time to check your work otherwise you may lose marks for lack of accuracy.

FESTIVALS AND CELEBRATIONS

¿Cuál es tu festival preferido? ¿Por qué?
What is your favourite festival? Why?

Mi fiesta preferida es la Nochevieja porque me quedo despierto/a toda la noche. El año pasado salimos a la medianoche para ver los fuegos artificiales. Lo pasé bomba.

My favourite festival is New Year's Eve because I get to stay up all night. Last year we went out at midnight to see the fireworks. I had a great time.

Describe una festividad que celebraste el año pasado.
Describe a festival that you celebrated last year.

Para Halloween, me disfracé de zombie y mi hermano menor tuvo mucho miedo. Hicimos 'trick or treat' y nuestros vecinos nos dieron un montón de caramelos. Fue una noche divertida.

For Halloween, I dressed up as a zombie and my little brother was very scared. We went trick or treating and our neighbours gave us lots of sweets. It was a fun night.

¿Qué piensas de las fiestas tradicionales?
What do you think of traditional festivals?

Estoy totalmente a favor de las fiestas tradicionales porque estas tradiciones nos permiten reunirnos con toda la familia y pasar tiempo juntos. A mi modo de ver, las fiestas representan las tradiciones de una región.

I am completely for traditional festivals because these traditions allow us to meet with all the family and spend time together. As I see it, festivals represent the traditions of a region.

¿Qué harás para celebrar tu próximo cumpleaños?
What will you do to celebrate your next birthday?

Celebraré mi cumpleaños con mis mejores amigos y mi familia. Mi madre me hará un pastel de cumpleaños y mi hermana organizará una fiesta en casa. ¡Espero recibir muchos regalos!
I will celebrate my birthday with my best friends and my family. My mum will make me a birthday cake and my sister will organise a house party. I hope to get lots of presents!

¿Te gustaría asistir a un festival de música?
Would you like to go to a music festival?

Nunca he asistido a un festival de música entonces después de mis exámenes, me gustaría ir a un festival de verano con mis amigos. Haremos camping allí y veremos a nuestros cantantes preferidos.
I've never been to a music festival, so after my exams I would like to go to a festival with my friends. We will camp there and we will see our favourite singers.

 GRAMMAR

Events taking place

To talk about an event taking place you can use tener lugar – e.g. la fiesta **tiene lugar** en verano (the party takes place/is held in summer).

The reflexive verb celebrarse is also used – this can mean 'to take place/to be held' – e.g. la conferencia **se celebra** en Madrid (the conference is held in Madrid) but it can also mean 'is celebrated' – e.g. la fiesta **se celebra** cada año (the party is celebrated every year).

You might sometimes see llevar(se) a cabo used. It literally means 'to carry out' but it can be used in the context of holding an event – e.g. el festival **se lleva a cabo** el miercóles (the festival is taking place on Wednesday).

 EXAM TASK

Translate the following paragraph into English:

El festival de música tuvo lugar el fin de semana pasado. Mis padres me dejaron ir con mis amigos por primera vez. Muchos turistas vinieron al pueblo para el evento y lo pasé fenomenal. Me encanta acampar y escuchar música en vivo y tengo ganas de volver al mismo festival el año que viene. ¡Va a ser increíble!

The translation into English is the last question on the reading exam and is worth 6 marks – this is only 2.5% of the whole GCSE so don't spend more time on it than you would on any other question on the reading paper.

FESTIVALS AND CELEBRATIONS

Las fiestas populares forman parte de nuestra cultura.	Popular festivals are part of our culture.
Lo más conocido mundialmente entre las tradiciones españolas son ciertamente el flamenco y las corridas de toros.	The most famous Spanish traditions worldwide are definitely flamenco dancing and bullfighting.
Estoy en contra de las corridas de toros.	I am against bullfighting.
Las fiestas locales fortalecen el sentido de comunidad.	Local festivals strengthen a sense of community.
Celebrar las tradiciones nos ayuda a mantenernos conectados a nuestra cultura.	Celebrating traditions helps to keep us connected to our culture.
Las fiestas son una excelente oportunidad para apreciar las culturas de todo el mundo.	Festivals are an excellent opportunity to appreciate cultures from all over the world.
No me gustan nada las sorpresas.	I don't like surprises at all.
Como a todo el mundo me encanta recibir regalos.	Like everyone, I love receiving presents.
Personalmente, me gusta más regalar que recibir regalos.	Personally, I prefer giving rather than receiving presents.
No sé cómo persuadir a mis padres para que me dejen ir solo/a a un festival.	I don't know how to persuade my parents to let me go to a festival on my own.
Cuando era pequeño/a, siempre celebraba mi cumpleaños con mi familia, pero ahora prefiero salir con mis amigos.	When I was younger, I always celebrated my birthday with my family, but now I prefer going out with my friends.
Tuve mucha suerte porque recibí un montón de regalos.	I was really lucky because I had loads of presents.
Decoramos la casa y siempre cenamos juntos.	We decorate the house and we always have dinner together.
Mi abuela siempre cocina una cena enorme.	My grandmother always cooks a huge dinner.
Mandar postales y tarjetas es una tradición que creo que merece la pena conservar.	Sending cards is a tradition that I think is worth keeping.
Antes prefería mi cumpleaños porque me gustaba recibir muchos regalos, pero ahora me gusta la Nochevieja porque mis amigos y yo podemos hacer una fiesta.	I used to prefer my birthday because I liked getting lots of presents, but now I like New Year's Eve because my friends and I can have a party.

Para mi cumpleaños me encantaría recibir un nuevo ordenador porque el mío está roto.	For my birthday I'd love to have a new computer as mine is broken.
Las fiestas españolas parecen muy divertidas e interesantes, por eso me encantaría ir a una fiesta en España.	Spanish festivals seem very fun and interesting, so I'd love to go to a festival in Spain.
Creo que mi fiesta española favorita es la Tomatina porque es muy diferente.	I think that my favourite Spanish festival is the Tomatina because it's very different.
Me gustaría participar en una fiesta española al menos una vez.	I would like to take part in a Spanish festival at least once.
Pienso que las tradiciones hacen la vida más interesante.	I think that traditions make life more interesting.
Para mí, las tradiciones son inútiles y no tienen ningún valor.	For me, traditions are useless and don't have any value.
Cada generación debería tener sus propias tradiciones.	Every generation should have its own traditions.
Mucha gente tiene puntos de vista diferentes sobre las fiestas.	Many people have different points of view about festivals.

GRAMMAR

Si sentences

Remember that you can use si (if) sentences to improve your Spanish.

You can use si + **present tense** followed by future tense (or immediate future) – e.g. **si tengo** suerte, recibiré muchos regalos (if I am lucky, I will receive lots of presents).

The more complex si sentence is si + **imperfect subjunctive** followed by conditional tense – e.g. **si tuviera** mucho dinero, tendría una fiesta enorme (if I had lots of money, I would have an enormous party).

For both of these constructions, you need to revise the future, immediate future and conditional tenses.

EXAM TASK

Answering conversation questions in writing on every topic is good revision practice for your writing exam too. Use and adapt the useful phrases on this page to help you answer the following. Remember to use a variety of tenses and to include more than one piece of information where possible. Can you justify your opinions?

- ¿Prefieres celebrar tu cumpleaños con tu familia o con tus amigos? ¿Por qué? Do you prefer celebrating your birthday with family or friends? Why?
- Los regalos son muy caros. ¿Qué piensas? Presents are very expensive. What do you think?
- Describe tu mejor cumpleaños. Describe your best birthday.
- ¿Cómo sería tu fiesta ideal? What would your ideal party be like?
- ¿Crees que las tradiciones culturales son importantes? ¿Por qué (no)? Do you think that cultural traditions are important? Why (not)?
- ¿Te gustan las fiestas? ¿Por qué (no)? Do you like festivals? Why (not)?
- ¿Cuál es tu fiesta preferida en tu país? ¿Por qué? What is your favourite festival in your country? Why?
- ¿Has asistido a un festival? Have you been to a festival?
- ¿Qué vas a hacer el próximo día festivo? What are you going to do next bank holiday?

LOCAL, NATIONAL, INTERNATIONAL AND GLOBAL AREAS OF INTEREST

HOME AND LOCALITY

The sub-theme of **Home and Locality** is divided into two areas. Here are some suggestions of topics to revise:

LOCAL AREAS OF INTEREST

- local facilities and amenities
- tourist attractions
- geographical features
- weather and climate
- advantages and disadvantages of where you live
- your local area in the past

TRANSPORT

- different types of transport
- advantages and disadvantages of types of transport
- different types of journey
- transport links
- buying tickets and booking a journey
- transport problems – e.g. delays, strikes, etc.

LETTER WRITING

You might have to write a letter or e-mail in your exam. Remember to use usted in a formal letter.

- In formal letters when you do not know the person, start with Muy señor/a mío/a or Estimado/a señor/a.
- If you know the name of the person, you can shorten Señor/Señora to Sr./Sra. – e.g. Estimado Sr. Pérez/Estimada Sra. González.

- If you are writing an informal letter or e-mail to a friend, use Querido/Querida/Queridos.
- End a formal letter with Le saluda atentamente or Atentamente.
- Slightly less formal endings are Un cordial saludo and Cordialmente.
- In friendly personal letters, you can end with Un (fuerte) abrazo or Con (todo mi) cariño.

LOCAL AREAS OF INTEREST

¿Qué piensas de tu región?
What do you think of your area?

Me gusta vivir aquí porque es una ciudad moderna y tiene de todo. Sin embargo, es muy sucia y ruidosa y hay mucha contaminación también. Preferiría vivir en el campo porque es menos industrial.
I like living here because it's a modern city and it has everything. However, it's very dirty and noisy and there is a lot of pollution as well. I would prefer to live in the countryside because it's less industrial.

¿Qué hay para los jóvenes en la zona en la que vives?
What is there for young people in your area?

No hay mucho que hacer para los jóvenes. Hay algunas tiendas y un cine bastante pequeño. Se puede jugar al tenis en el parque, pero creo que necesitamos un polideportivo.
There isn't much for young people to do. There are some shops and quite a small cinema. You can play tennis in the park, but I think we need a leisure centre.

¿Qué vas a hacer en tu región este fin de semana?
What are you going to do in your area this weekend?

Voy a salir con mis amigos al centro de la ciudad e iremos al cine. Por desgracia, mi ciudad no tiene muchas atracciones entonces no hay mucho que podemos hacer los fines de semana.
I'm going to go out with my friends in the town centre and we will go to the cinema. Unfortunately, my town doesn't have many attractions so there isn't much that we can do at the weekend.

¿Cómo era tu barrio en el pasado?
What was your area like in the past?

Mis abuelos me dijeron que la ciudad tenía menos industria y una población más pequeña. Había más parques y espacios verdes y la ciudad era más tranquila. Hoy en día hay muchas fábricas y el aire está contaminado.
My grandparents told me that the town had less industry and a smaller population. There were more parks and green spaces and the town was quieter. Nowadays, there are lots of factories and the air is polluted.

¿Qué te gustaría cambiar de tu barrio?

What would you like to change in your area?

Me gustaría cambiar muchas cosas porque no tenemos una piscina ni una bolera. En mi opinión, hacen falta más instalaciones deportivas. También haría algo para mejorar el centro comercial porque no tiene tiendas muy buenas.

I would like to change lots of things because we don't have a swimming pool or a bowling alley. In my opinion, we need more sports facilities. I would also do something to improve the shopping centre because it doesn't have very good shops.

 It doesn't matter if you live in a huge, vibrant city or a tiny village miles from anywhere. You can make up details if you need to – no one is going to come round to check whether what you have said or written is true! As well as being able to describe your local area, you need to offer opinions and discuss advantages and disadvantages.

GRAMMAR

Talking about your town

To say what there is in your town, use **hay** (there is/there are) – e.g. **hay** muchas tiendas (there are lots of shops). To say what there was, or what there used to be in the past, use **había** (there was/there were) – e.g. en el pasado **había** menos tráfico (in the past there was less traffic).

You might also need to use the imperfect tense to say what your town or local area was like in the past – e.g. mi pueblo **era** más tranquilo (my village was quieter). You can also use it to say what you used to do regularly in your local area – e.g. **en el pasado jugaba** en el parque (in the past I used to play in the park).

EXAM TASK

Lee la información sobre el centro de la ciudad. Empareja 1–4 con la letra correcta.

1. Los grandes centros comerciales suelen abrir hasta las 21.00 o 22.00 cada día menos el domingo, que cierran a las 17.00.
2. Están abiertos de 9.30 a 16.30 para sacar dinero y algunos también abren los sábados por la mañana.
3. Allí se pueden comprar sellos, enviar paquetes, pagar las facturas de electricidad, teléfono, etc.
4. Sirven comida hasta las 22.00–23.00 y tienen ofertas especiales para la comida entre las 11.00 y las 14.00.

a. La oficina de correos
b. Los museos
c. Las tiendas
d. Los restaurantes
e. Los hospitales
f. Los bancos

Be careful with this common type of question. Distractors are harder to spot in Spanish! There are two answers which you won't need to use – look out for keywords to help you match up the correct number and letter.

LOCAL AREAS OF INTEREST

Me parece que hay mucha cultura en mi zona. Por ejemplo, se puede visitar el castillo y la cathedral.

It seems to me that there's a lot of culture in my region. For example, you can visit the castle and the cathedral.

Siempre me ha gustado vivir aquí porque mis vecinos son encantadores y hay mucha gente de mi edad.

I have always liked living here because my neighbours are lovely and there are lots of people my age.

Vivo en mi barrio desde que nací y siempre he vivido en la misma casa.

I have lived in my area since I was born and I've always lived in the same house.

Solo llevo un año viviendo en este barrio desde que nos mudamos recientemente.

I've only been living in this area for a year since we moved recently.

Hay muchas ventajas y desventajas de vivir en mi barrio; por ejemplo …

There are lots of advantages and disadvantages of living in my area; for example …

Para divertirse hay una variedad de restaurantes, bares y discotecas.

For leisure, there's a variety of restaurants, bars and discos.

En mi opinión, es esencial mejorar la red de transporte público.

In my opinion it's essential to improve the public transport network.

Deberíamos construir una zona peatonal porque hay demasiado tráfico.

We should build a pedestrian zone because there is too much traffic.

Mi barrio es conocido por su equipo de fútbol y el año que viene van a construir un estadio nuevo.

My area is known for its football team and next year they are going to build a new stadium.

No hay absolutamente nada de interés en mi barrio porque está en las afueras de la ciudad.

There is absolutely nothing of interest in my area because it's on the outskirts of the city.

En el pasado había mucha industria y fábricas, pero ahora hay mucho paro.

In the past there was a lot of industry and many factories but now there is a lot of unemployment.

Creo que el centro de la ciudad es peligroso y necesitamos cámaras de seguridad en las calles.

I think that the town centre is dangerous and that we need security cameras in the streets.

Si fuera alcalde/alcaldesa construiría más casas baratas para la población creciente.

If I were the mayor, I would build more cheap houses for the growing population.

Mi pueblo está lejos del centro de la ciudad y no hay autobuses regulares, entonces estamos bastante aislados.

My village is far from the city centre and there aren't regular buses, so we are quite isolated.

Preferiría vivir en un pueblo porque me gustaría formar parte de una comunidad.

I would prefer to live in a village because I would like to be part of a community.

Es muy aburrido vivir aquí porque no hay nada que hacer y todos mis amigos viven muy lejos de mí. ¡Lo odio!	It's very boring living here because there is nothing to do and all my friends live very far away from me. I hate it!
A mí me gusta mi región a pesar de que donde yo vivo no hay mucho que hacer.	I like my region even though where I live there isn't much to do.
Mi ciudad es bastante moderna porque fue construida en los años 70.	My city is quite modern because it was built in the 1970s.
Mi barrio es una mezcla de antiguo y moderno y tiene una historia bastante interesante.	My area is a mix of old and modern and it has quite an interesting history.

GRAMMAR

Your local area

To say what you can do in your area use **se puede + infinitive** – e.g. **se puede ir** al cine (you can go to the cinema), **se puede visitar** los monumentos (you can visit the monuments).

There are also different ways to talk about what your local area needs.

You can use the verb necesitar – e.g. mi ciudad **necesita** más tiendas (my town/city needs more shops).

Or you can use hacer falta, which works in exactly the same way as gustar – e.g. you could say nos **hace falta** un centro comercial (we need a shopping centre) or a mi ciudad le **hacen falta** más restaurantes (my town/city needs more restaurants).

EXAM TASK

Translate the following paragraph into Spanish:

I like living in my town because there are lots of things for young people to do. In the past there wasn't a cinema, but now there is a big shopping centre near the river. In my opinion, we need more buses. In the future, I would like to live in Spain because I love Spanish culture and it's sunny.

Check carefully that you are using the correct tenses.

TRANSPORT

¿Cuál es tu medio de transporte preferido? ¿Por qué?
What is your favourite type of transport? Why?

Prefiero viajar en avión porque es más cómodo y relajante que
el tren. El avión es el medio de transporte más seguro que existe
y la posibilidad de sufrir un accidente en avión es mínima.
I prefer travelling by plane as it's comfortable and relaxing.
The plane is the safest method of transport that exists and the
possibility of having an accident is minimal.

¿Cuáles son las ventajas y desventajas del transporte público?
What are the advantages and disadvantages of public transport?

Primero, el transporte público reduce el número de vehículos en las carreteras y,
por lo tanto, es beneficioso para el medio ambiente. Es barato y práctico, pero
hay que admitir que no es muy cómodo. A veces no hay asientos y siempre hay
retrasos.
Firstly, public transport reduces the number of vehicles on the road and therefore
it's beneficial for the environment. It's cheap and practical but you have to admit
it's not very comfortable. Sometimes there are no seats and there are always delays.

¿Cuáles son los inconvenientes de viajar en coche?
What are the disadvantages of travelling by car?

La verdad es que el coche ofrece bastantes desventajas serias; por ejemplo, el alto
precio de la gasolina. Aparcar en el centro de la ciudad es imposible, siempre hay
atascos y el coche produce mucha contaminación. Sin embargo, el coche te da
libertad y, como todos mis amigos, tengo la intención de aprender a conducir.
The truth is that the car has quite a few serious disadvantages; for example, the
high price of petrol. Parking in the city centre is impossible, there are always traffic
jams and cars emit a lot of pollution. Nevertheless, a car gives you freedom and,
like all my friends, I intend to learn to drive.

¿Cómo fuiste al colegio ayer?
How did you get to school yesterday?

Normalmente voy al colegio a pie porque no está lejos, pero llovió ayer por la mañana entonces fui en coche con mis vecinos.
Normally I go to school on foot because it's not far, but it rained yesterday morning so I went by car with my neighbours.

¿Como viajarás de vacaciones el año que viene?
How will you travel for your holiday next year?

El verano que viene iré a Francia con mi familia y viajaremos en coche y en barco. Me encanta el ferry porque hay mucho que hacer durante el viaje.
Next summer I will go to France with my family and we will travel by car and boat. I love the ferry because there are lots of things to do during the journey.

EXAM TASK

Read the literary text and answer the questions in English.
Veía la tele cuando escuché el ruido. Salí afuera para saber qué había ocurrido. Habían colisionado dos coches. Y allí estaba, era el coche de Mateo. Distinguiría el coche de Mateo en cualquier lugar porque lo compramos juntos el año pasado. Comencé a correr. Al llegar, abrí la puerta y le ayudé a salir.

1. What was the author doing when she heard the noise?
2. What had happened to cause the noise?
3. Why was she able to recognise Mateo's car?
4. What did she do once she reached the car?

GRAMMAR

Adjectives
• Don't forget that adjectives need to have different endings depending on whether you are describing a masculine, feminine, singular or plural noun – e.g. el coche es **pequeño** (the car is small), la estación es **moderna** (the station is modern), los trenes son **rápidos** (the trains are fast).
• To make comparisons between different types of transport, use más … que or menos … que – e.g. el tren es **más** cómodo **que** el autobús (the train is more comfortable than the bus), el metro es **menos** caro **que** el tranvía (the metro is less expensive than the tram).
• But if you want to say better or worse, then you use mejor que or peor que – e.g. viajar en avión es **mejor que** ir en tren (travelling by plane is better than going by train).

This text is mainly written in the past tense.
The first sentence (veía la tele cuando escuché el ruido) is a good example of the difference between the imperfect and the preterite tense. The imperfect is used to describe something that was happening at the time (**veía** la tele) and the preterite is used to talk about a single completed event (**escuché** el ruido).

TRANSPORT

Odio esperar en la parada de autobús.	I hate waiting at the bus stop.
Siempre me mareo en el coche.	I always get car sick.
Preferiría viajar en coche, pero hay que pensar en el medio ambiente.	I would prefer to travel by car, but you have to think of the environment.
En mi opinión, los autobuses son demasiados lentos.	In my opinion, buses are too slow.
Ir en bicicleta es más sano y práctico.	Going by bike is more healthy and practical.
El transporte público es sucio e incómodo.	Public transport is dirty and uncomfortable.
Prefiero ir al colegio andando porque me da independencia.	I prefer to walk to school because it gives me independence.
Puedo leer una revista cuando viajo en tren.	I can read a magazine when I travel by train.
Hay demasiados retrasos.	There are too many delays.
Viajar en coche es más rápido, ya que evitas trasbordos y llegas directamente a tu destino.	Travelling by car is quicker, as you avoid changes and you arrive directly at your destination.
El transporte público es la alternativa más ecológica para los desplazamientos que se hacen en la ciudad.	Public transport is the most ecological alternative for journeys in town.
Usar el transporte público resulta más barato que el vehículo privado.	Using public transport is cheaper than a private vehicle.
Con el transporte público llegas a tu destino sin complicaciones y sin estrés.	With public transport you arrive at your destination without complications and without stress.
Nunca queda un asiento libre en las horas punta.	There's never a free seat at rush hour.
Los aeropuertos son muy aburridos y el tiempo de espera antes y después del vuelo es bastante largo y tedioso.	Airports are very boring and the waiting time before and after the flight is quite long and tedious.
La seguridad en los aeropuertos es muy exigente.	The security in airports is very demanding.
Una de las cosas que menos me gusta de viajar es el tiempo de espera.	One of the things I like least about travelling is the waiting time.
En mi pueblo, la frecuencia de los autobuses es muy escasa.	In my village the buses are very infrequent.
Los trenes son mucho más ecológicos que cualquier otro transporte porque pueden transportar a cientos de pasajeros.	Trains are more ecological than any other form of transport because they can transport hundreds of passengers.

El precio de los billetes debería ser más económico y accesible.

The price of tickets should be cheaper and more affordable.

Los coches son costosos para comprar y mantener, sin mencionar el alto costo de la gasolina.

Cars are costly to buy and maintain, without mentioning the high cost of petrol.

This topic isn't just about buying a ticket!
You need to be able to give opinions on different types of transport and make comparisons between them. What are the advantages and disadvantages of different types of transport? Think of ways to include past, present and future tenses in your answers.

GRAMMAR

Adverbs
You might need to use adverbs when talking about transport and journeys in Spanish. Adverbs are used to express how, when, where or to what extent something is happening. Many Spanish adverbs are formed by adding **mente** to the feminine adjective – e.g.:

> rápida (quick) → rápida**mente** (quickly)
> lenta (slow) → lenta**mente** (slowly)

Some adverbs don't follow this pattern – e.g. **bien** (well), **mal** (badly), **a menudo** (often), **a veces** (sometimes).
    You can also make comparisons with adverbs using **más ... que** and **menos ... que** – e.g. llego **menos** rápidamente en tren **que** en autobús (I arrive less quickly by train than by bus).

In the speaking exam, the first question on the photo card will ask you to describe the photo (or what is happening in it):

- Describe la foto. (Foundation)/¿De qué trata esta foto? (Higher)

The second question will usually ask you for an opinion – e.g.:

- ¿Crees que es peligroso ir en bicicleta por las carreteras? ¿Por qué (no)? Do you think it's dangerous cycling on roads? Why (not)?

Your teacher will then ask you **two** unseen questions. In the first unseen question, you will usually have to comment on an opinion – e.g.:

- El transporte público es demasiado caro. ¿Estás de acuerdo? Public transport is too expensive. Do you agree?

The last question will usually need to be answered in a different tense – e.g.:

- ¿Que tipos de transporte utilizaste la semana pasada? Which types of transport did you use last week?

In your preparation time, try to think of some of the things you might be asked in the unseen questions.

LOCAL, NATIONAL, INTERNATIONAL AND GLOBAL AREAS OF INTEREST

SPAIN AND SPANISH-SPEAKING COUNTRIES

The sub-theme of **Spain and Spanish-Speaking Countries** is divided into two areas. Here are some suggestions of topics to revise:

LOCAL AND REGIONAL FEATURES AND CHARACTERISTICS

- places of interest in Spanish-speaking countries
- geographical features
- weather and climate
- tourist attractions and monuments
- regional characteristics

HOLIDAYS AND TOURISM

- holiday locations and resorts
- types of holiday
- holiday accommodation
- holiday activities
- advantages and disadvantages of tourism
- different types of tourism
- problems and complaints

REMEMBER:

Remember that you will be marked for linguistic knowledge and accuracy in your speaking and writing exams. It is important to spend time revising basic things like:

- genders of nouns
- verb endings
- adjectives (and agreements)
- prepositions
- tenses

When revising this topic you are not expected to be an expert on every tourist attraction in Spain, but you should be able to talk generally about the topic.

LOCAL AND REGIONAL FEATURES AND CHARACTERISTICS

¿Has visitado España alguna vez?
Have you ever visited Spain?

Nunca he visitado España, pero tengo ganas de ir a Barcelona para ver el estadio Camp Nou. Mis abuelos fueron a la Costa del Sol el verano pasado y dijeron que las playas eran muy bonitas.
I've never visited Spain, but I'm keen to go to Barcelona to see the Camp Nou stadium. My grandparents went to the Costa del Sol last summer and they said the beaches were very pretty.

¿Te gusta visitar monumentos históricos durante tus vacaciones? ¿Por qué (no)?
Do you like visiting historical monuments during your holiday? Why (not)?

Creo que es importante aprender un poco de la historia de una región durante las vacaciones, pero tengo que admitir que encuentro los museos bastante aburridos. Lo que realmente me gusta es comer comida local y comprar recuerdos.
I think it's important to learn a bit about the history of an area during your holiday, but I have to admit that I find museums quite boring. What I really like is eating local food and buying souvenirs.

¿Qué país hispanohablante te gustaría visitar? ¿Por qué?
Which Spanish-speaking country would you like to visit? Why?

Me gustaría visitar México porque las playas son hermosas y los hoteles son lujosos. También, me encantaría visitar todos los sitios de interés. Tendría que ahorrar mucho dinero porque es caro viajar allí.
I would like to visit Mexico because the beaches are beautiful and the hotels are luxurious. Also, I would love to visit all of the places of interest. I would have to save a lot of money because it's expensive to travel there.

If you've never been to Spain or a Spanish-speaking country you can either make up a visit so you've got something to talk about or describe where you'd like to visit! Remember to justify your opinions and give reasons. There is a lot of overlap with the vocabulary you need for **local areas of interest**, just in a different context.

Describe una visita que hiciste recientemente a una atracción turística.
Describe a recent visit you made to a tourist attraction.

El fin de semana pasado, hicimos una excursión al castillo. Había un montón de turistas, pero lo pasamos bien.
Last weekend, we went on a trip to the castle. There were loads of tourists but we had a good time.

¿Es importante aprender sobre la cultura de una región durante las vacaciones? ¿Por qué (no)?
Is it important to learn about the history of an area when you're on holiday? Why (not)?

Pienso que los turistas deberían respetar las diferentes culturas, pero no es esencial visitar los museos y los monumentos. Personalmente, prefiero combinar la cultura y el descanso durante mis vacaciones.
I think that tourists should respect different cultures, but it's not essential to visit museums and monuments. Personally, I prefer to combine culture and relaxation during my holidays.

GRAMMAR

Prepositions

Some key prepositions to talk about location include:

delante de – in front of
detrás de – behind
enfrente de – opposite
a la derecha de – to the right of
a la izquierda de – to the left of
al lado de – next to
al final de – at the end of
lejos (de) – far (from)
cerca (de) – near (to)

Remember to use **estar** with all of these – e.g. **el museo está** al lado del cine (the museum is next to the cinema), **la oficina está** al final de la calle (the office is at the end of the road).

EXAM TASK

Translate the following paragraph into English:

El castillo es un destino turístico muy popular y se encuentra en el centro de la ciudad a la derecha del parque. Está abierto todos los días desde las diez y la entrada es gratuita los domingos y días festivos. Fui al monumento ayer y fue muy educativo. Para mí es muy importante descubrir la cultura y la historia de una región. Mañana me gustaría visitar el museo.

Make sure you check that your English makes sense. Don't forget that the word order could be different in Spanish.

LOCAL AND REGIONAL FEATURES AND CHARACTERISTICS

Para mí es muy importante descubrir la cultura y la historia de un destino turístico.	For me, it's very important to discover the culture and history of a tourist destination.
Si tenemos la oportunidad de viajar a países diferentes, aprenderemos sobre otras maneras de vivir.	If we have the opportunity to travel to different countries, we will learn about other ways of living.
Creo que viajar al extranjero puede ayudar a eliminar el racismo y los prejuicios.	I think that travelling abroad can help to eliminate racism and prejudices.
A mi modo de ver, lo más importante es intentar expresarse en el idioma del país.	As I see it, the most important thing is to try to express yourself in the language of the country.
España es muy conocida por la música y el baile, las corridas de toros, las playas fantásticas y, por supuesto, el sol.	Spain is very well known for music and dancing, bullfighting, fantastic beaches and, of course, the sun.
España es uno de los centros culturales de Europa y tiene mucho que ofrecer.	Spain is one of the cultural centres of Europe and has a lot to offer.
La Sagrada Familia de Barcelona es el monumento más conocido y característico de la ciudad.	The Sagrada Familia in Barcelona is the most famous and characteristic monument in the city.
Desde un punto de vista cultural, los países sudamericanos me fascinan.	From a cultural point of view, South American countries fascinate me.
Si tuviera la oportunidad, me encantaría visitar América del Sur.	If I had the opportunity, I would love to visit South America.
Machu Picchu es uno de los sitios arqueológicos más interesantes del planeta.	Machu Picchu is one of the most interesting archeological sites on the planet.
Es una ciudad histórica con una riqueza cultural muy grande y sería una experiencia inolvidable viajar allí.	It's a historical city with a very rich culture and it would be an unforgettable experience to travel there.
Los parques temáticos son unos de los destinos favoritos en la temporada estival.	The theme parks are one of the favourite destinations in the summer season.
La ciudad ofrece numerosas actividades culturales y gastronómicas.	The city offers numerous cultural and gastronomical activities.
Me gustaría tener la oportunidad de disfrutar de la amplia oferta cultural de la ciudad.	I would like to have the opportunity to enjoy the vast cultural offerings of the city.

Es un país con una gran historia y es uno de los principales destinos turísticos del mundo.

It's a country with a great history and it's one of the principal tourist destinations in the world.

Se pueden visitar muchos edificios antiguos que representan la historia y la tradición del país.

You can visit many old buildings that represent the history and traditions of the country.

GRAMMAR

Hacer

In Spanish, you use the verb hacer with most weather phrases:

hace buen/mal tiempo – it is good/bad weather
hace calor/frío/sol/viento – it is hot/cold/sunny/windy

If you want to describe what the weather was like during your holiday, you will need to use the imperfect tense – **hacía** calor etc.
Some other useful weather phrases include:

llueve – it is raining
llovía – it was raining
nieva – it is snowing
nevaba – it was snowing
está despejado/nublado – it is clear/cloudy
estaba despejado/nublado – it was clear/cloudy
hay niebla/tormenta – there is fog/a storm
había niebla/tormenta – there was fog/a storm

Sometimes you will see weather expressions in the preterite tense as well – this is used to describe weather at a specific point in time. Key verbs for this are hizo, llovió, nevó, estuvo and hubo.

EXAM TASK

Here are some examples of role play prompts on this topic. One bullet point will ask for **two** details, pieces of information or opinions. Make sure you plan **two** things to say during your preparation time.

- El clima (**dos** detalles)
- Actividades (**dos** detalles)
- ? una atracción turística
- ? el precio – una actividad
- España – una visita – el año pasado
- Los monumentos – el año que viene

For the first bullet point you could say something as simple as Hace calor y hace sol or you could use two separate sentences – e.g. Hace frío. Llueve.

HOLIDAYS AND TOURISM

¿Qué haces normalmente durante las vacaciones?
What do you normally do during the holidays?

Normalmente voy de vacaciones con mis padres y nos quedamos en un camping. Hacemos muchas cosas divertidas y visitamos muchos sitios de interés. Suelo pasarlo bastante bien pero este verano iré a Francia con mis amigos.
Normally I go on holiday with my parents and we stay in a campsite. We do lots of fun things and we visit lots of places of interest. I usually have quite a good time but this summer I will go to France with my friends.

¿Cuáles son los aspectos negativos del turismo?
What are the negative aspects of tourism?

Pues, el desarrollo turístico trae consigo varios problemas. Algunos turistas se comportan mal y no respetan las costumbres de los que viven en la zona. La construcción de hoteles y complejos turísticas destruye el entorno natural y aumenta el coste de la vivienda para los habitantes locales.
Well, tourist development brings with it various problems. Some tourists behave badly and don't respect the customs of those who live in the area. Building hotels and tourist complexes destroys the natural world and increases the cost of housing for local residents.

¿Qué tipo de vacaciones prefieres? ¿Por qué?
What type of holidays do you prefer? Why?

Prefiero la playa porque me gusta la natación y todos los deportes acuáticos. Es importante para mí hacer nuevas cosas durante las vacaciones; por ejemplo, el año pasado aprendí a hacer windsurf.
I prefer the beach because I like swimming and all water sports. It's important for me to do new things on holiday; for example, last year I learned to windsurf.

¿Qué hiciste el verano pasado?
What did you do last summer?

El verano pasado hice muchas cosas. Primero fui a la costa con mis padres, mi hermana y mis abuelos. Estuvimos allí un mes entero y me lo pasé muy bien bañándome en el mar y haciendo pequeñas excursiones. Unos amigos míos estaban también de vacaciones allí y fuimos con ellos a un restaurante.
Last summer I did a lot of things. First, I went to the coast with my parents, my sister and my grandparents. We were there for a whole month and I had a really good time swimming in the sea and going on little trips. Some friends of mine were also on holiday there and we went with them to a restaurant.

¿Cómo serían tus vacaciones de sueño?

What would your dream holiday be like?

Si tuviera muchísimo dinero, iría a una isla tropical con toda mi familia. Viajaríamos en primera clase, por supuesto. Haría sol todos los días y las playas serian increíbles con arena blanca y mar turquesa. Nos quedaríamos en un hotel de cinco estrellas que tendría una piscina enorme.

If I had lots of money, I would go to a tropical island with my family. We would travel first class, of course. It would be sunny every day and the beaches would be incredible with white sand and turquoise sea. We would stay in a five-star hotel, which would have an enormous swimming pool.

You should feel confident about using the past, present and future tenses in your spoken and written Spanish.

You can also add in a variety of other tenses and expressions to extend your answers. For example:

- The present tense to talk about activities you do regularly – e.g. voy a la playa.
- The present continuous to say what you are doing at the time of speaking – e.g. estoy leyendo un libro.
- The preterite to talk about something you did – e.g. fui a la discoteca.
- The imperfect tense for things that used to happen regularly in the past – e.g. hacía sol.
- The perfect tense to say what you have done – e.g. he visitado el castillo.
- The pluperfect tense to say what you had done – e.g. había hecho muchas actividades.
- The immediate future to say what you are going to do – e.g. voy a ir de vacaciones.
- The future tense to say what you will do – e.g. viajaré al extranjero.
- The conditional tense to say what you would do – e.g. me quedaría en un hotel de lujo.

You don't have to use all of these tenses in each answer, but you need to be able to recognise them as they will appear in listening and reading exercises. You will need to refer to past, present and future events in your speaking and writing exams.

EXAM TASK

Lee lo que dicen estos jóvenes sobre sus vacaciones ideales. Escribe la letra correcta para cada persona.

Rita: Mis vacaciones ideales **serían** en un hotel de cinco estrellas.

Miguel: Me gustaría descubrir otras culturas y tradiciones.

Xavi: Odio las actividades físicas, **preferiría** broncearme en la playa todos los días.

Marina: Me encantaría estar en plena naturaleza y dormir al aire libre.

a. prefiere hacer camping
b. quiere comprar recuerdos
c. prefiere el alojamiento de lujo
d. le encanta visitar los sitios de interés
e. nada cada día
f. siempre toma el sol

Be careful – there are two extra answers here to distract you! These four young people are talking about their ideal holidays, so they are all using the conditional tense (the verbs have been highlighted in bold for you).

HOLIDAYS AND TOURISM

Se dice que las vacaciones son fundamentales para mantener una buena salud física y mental.

They say holidays are fundamental for maintaning good mental and physical health.

En general prefiero las vacaciones activas porque soy una persona deportista.

In general, I prefer active holidays because I am a sporty person.

Creo que las vacaciones de sol y playa son una pérdida de tiempo.

I think that beach holidays are a waste of time.

Pasé una semana visitando todas las atracciones turísticas y el año que viene me gustaría volver al mismo sitio.

I spent a week visiting all the tourist attractions and next year I'd like to go back to the same place.

No es esencial que las vacaciones sean largas y costosas.

It's not essential that holidays are long and expensive.

Para conseguir mis vacaciones ideales, necesitaría mucho dinero.

In order to have my ideal holiday, I would need a lot of money.

No me gusta quedarme en alojamientos de baja calidad, pero la verdad es que no tengo mucho dinero.

I don't like staying in low quality accommodation, but the truth is that I don't have much money.

Preferiría conocer países menos desarrollados y saber en que situación se encuentran.

I would prefer to get to know less developed countries and find out what situation they are in.

Las vacaciones ayudan a reducir estrés y salir de la rutina.

Holidays help to reduce stress and are a break from routine.

Para mí, las vacaciones me ayudan a acercarme a mi familia porque siempre regresamos felices.

For me, holidays help me get closer to my family because we always come back happy.

Es evidente que el turismo es una importante fuente de ingresos para el país.

It's clear that tourism is an important source of income for the country.

Muchos viajeros extranjeros se comportan mal durante sus vacaciones.

Many foreign travellers behave badly during their holidays.

España es una de los principales destinos turísticos de Europa.

Spain is one of the principal tourist destinations in Europe.

Se han construido más carreteras, hoteles y aeropuertos.

They have built more roads, hotels and airports.

A pesar de las ventajas, el turismo tiene muchas desventajas.

Despite the advantages, tourism has many disadvantages.

A mi modo de ver, el turismo está destruyendo la cultura y las tradiciones.

As I see it, tourism is destroying culture and traditions.

Por otro lado, el turismo tiene un efecto positivo en la economía del país y crea muchos empleos.

El turismo en algunos lugares tiene una reputación muy negativa, debido a la falta de respeto de los turistas.

On the other hand, tourism has a positive impact on the economy of a country and it creates many jobs.

Tourism in some places has a very negative reputation due to tourists' lack of respect.

GRAMMAR

Complete the following paragraph using the correct verb in either the present, preterite or future tense.

Normalmente _____ de vacaciones con mis padres y _____ en un camping. Lo _____ bastante bien, pero este verano _____ a Francia con mis amigos. _____ en barco y _____ en un albergue. El año pasado _____ a Alemania con mi colegio. _____ muchas cosas divertidas y _____ muchos sitios de interés. En general _____ las vacaciones activas porque _____una persona deportista.

nos quedaremos	**soy**
nos quedamos	**hicimos**
prefiero	**iré**
paso	**visitamos**
fui	**voy**
viajaremos	

EXAM TASK

Escribe sobre tus vacaciones. Tienes que escribir una frase completa en español sobre:

- el transporte
- el alojamiento
- el clima
- la comida
- las actividades
- tus opiniones

Make sure your sentence is complete and contains an appropriate verb – e.g. for the first bullet point you should say **voy en avión** not just **en avión**.

LOCAL, NATIONAL, INTERNATIONAL AND GLOBAL AREAS OF INTEREST

GLOBAL SUSTAINABILITY

The sub-theme of **Global Sustainability** is divided into two areas. Here are some suggestions of topics to revise:

ENVIRONMENT

- environmental issues
- recycling
- climate change
- drought and flooding
- pollution
- types of energy
- environmental groups

SOCIAL ISSUES

- charity events
- raising money
- worldwide problems – e.g. poverty, famine, health, homelessness
- volunteering

ADVICE

A task on the environment or social issues might seem harder than some of the other sub-themes. You will need to learn some topic-specific vocabulary but the expectations are the same as with all the other sub-themes. You need to express opinions and refer to events using the past, present and future tenses. Try to write extended sentences using connectives. You can combine more than one tense in a sentence and you can vary the vocabulary that you use to express opinions. Revise how you could do the following:

- express which social or environmental problems you are worried about and why
- talk about a charity you support and what it does
- talk about something that happened in the past – e.g. a charity event you attended
- say what you do at the moment to support charities or help the environment
- talk about a future event – e.g. a cake sale you will organise, a fundraiser you will attend, your plans to volunteer, how you will become more eco-friendly, etc.
- say how young people can help or what people should do to help

ENVIRONMENT

¿Crees que es importante reciclar? ¿Por qué (no)?
Do you think recycling is important? Why (not)?

Claro que sí, es importantísimo reciclar para proteger el futuro de nuestro planeta. Sobre todo, es necesario separar la basura y reciclar lo más posible para conservar los recursos naturales.
Of course, recycling is really important to protect the future of our planet. Above all, it's necessary to separate rubbish and recycle as much as possible in order to save natural resources.

Describe la última cosa que hiciste para ayudar al medioambiente.
Describe the last thing you did to help the environment.

Esta mañana me duché en vez de bañarme para ahorrar dinero y no malgastar el agua. También comí productos locales en el desayuno.
This morning I had a shower instead of a bath to save money and not waste water. Also I ate local products for breakfast.

¿Te consideras una persona ecologista? ¿Por qué (no)?
Do you consider yourself to be eco-friendly? Why (not)?

Hago todo lo que puedo, pero no soy perfecto/a. Es bastante difícil renunciar a los productos no biodegradables, pero intento utilizar más productos naturales y menos productos químicos.
I do all I can but I'm not perfect. It's quite difficult to give up non-biodegradable products, but I try to use more natural products and fewer chemical products.

¿Piensas que todos somos responsables del cuidado del medio ambiente? ¿Por qué (no)?
Do you think we are all responsible for caring for the environment? Why (not)?

Pienso que el gobierno debería hacer más para educar y formar a la gente, pero la verdad es que tenemos que modificar muchos aspectos de nuestro comportamiento para proteger el medio ambiente. Todos debemos cuidar de nuestro alrededor y contribuir a un planeta sostenible.
I think that the government should do more to educate and train people, but the truth is that we have to modify many aspects of our behaviour to protect the environment. We must all care for our surroundings and contribute to a sustainable planet.

¿Qué se debería hacer para proteger el medioambiente?
What should we do to protect the environment?

Hay muchas cosas que se deberían hacer, pero en mi opinión lo más importante es consumir energía de manera responsable. En casa, deberiamos bajar la temperatura de la calefacción central y apagar las luces para ahorrar la electricidad.
There are many things we should do, but in my opinion the most important is using energy responsibly. At home, we should reduce the temperature of the central heating and switch off lights to save electricity.

The following are useful verbs for talking about the environment. Can you translate them into English? Can you write a sentence using each one? Vary your tenses where possible.

- ayudar
- proteger
- respetar
- salvar
- mejorar
- reciclar
- contaminar
- limpiar
- destrozar
- dañar

GRAMMAR

Deber
In this topic, typical questions might ask you for solutions to problems or about things we should do to help the environment. You need to use the verb deber in the conditional tense to express this – e.g. **deberíamos** tomar medidas urgentes (we should take urgent measures).

Match the name to each statement.
Ismael: A mi modo de ver, muchas personas no consumen energía de manera responsable.

Lena: Considero que es imprescindible[1] construir casas y colegios ecológicos.

Oli: Mi opinión personal es que el gobierno debería hacer más para promover[2] las energías renovables.

Zaca: Es ridículo que la gente prefiera quedarse sentada en un atasco[3] que ir a pie.

Iván: Me parece triste que haya tanta contaminación en las grandes ciudades.

Antonio: Hay que animar a la gente a apagar[4] las luces y no dejar los equipos en modo de espera.

1. essential   2. promote   3. traffic jam   4. switch off

Who …
1. is concerned about pollution?
2. thinks that people should save electricity?
3. thinks that we need more environmentally friendly buildings?
4. wants the government to do more?
5. thinks people waste energy?
6. thinks people should use their cars less?

These statements are all great examples of how to express complex opinions on this topic. It's important to think of different ways to express your opinion rather than just say how often you recycle! This sub-theme allows you to really show off your linguistic skills – if you have strong opinions then learn how to express them! Some other good phrases are:

Tengo que decir/reconocer/admitir que … – I have to say/recognise/admit that …
Es innegable que … – It's undeniable that …

If you are a bit less sure of your opinions on a topic, you could say:

Supongo/imagino que … – I suppose/imagine that …
Es difícil dar una opinión, pero … – It's difficult to give an opinion, but …
Es un tema muy complejo, pero … – It's a very complicated subject, but …

ENVIRONMENT

USEFUL
PHRASES

Pienso que deberíamos ser más conscientes de los problemas medioambientales.	I think we should be more aware of environmental problems.
Me preocupan mucho las especies en peligro de extinción.	I'm very worried about endangered species.
Todos tenemos que poner nuestro granito de arena.	We all have to do our bit.
Llevo mis propias bolsas siempre conmigo y rechazo las bolsas de plástico.	I always take my own bags with me and decline plastic bags.
Cuando era pequeño/a no reciclaba mucho pero ahora siempre lo hago.	When I was younger I didn't recycle much but now I always do it.
La lucha contra el cambio climático es responsabilidad de todo el mundo.	The fight against climate change is everyone's responsibility.
El calentamiento global es causado por la acción humana.	Global warming is caused by human actions.
Si apagáramos la calefacción central, ahorraríamos mucha energía.	If we switched off the heating, we would save a lot of energy.
Hay muchas cosas que podemos hacer si queremos ser ecológicos.	There are many things we can do if we want to be environmentally friendly.
Tenemos que ser conscientes que el agua es un recurso que se agota.	We have to be aware that water is a resource that is running out.
Todos sabemos la importancia que tiene reciclar para nuestro planeta.	We all know the importance of recycling for our planet.
Hay demasiado tráfico y siempre hay basura en el suelo.	There is too much traffic and there is always rubbish on the floor.
Hace diez años había menos contaminación del aire y las calles estaban limpias.	Ten years ago there was less air pollution and the streets were clean.
Si no cuidamos el planeta, tendremos más desastres ecológicos en el futuro.	If we don't care for the planet, we will have more ecological disasters in the future.
La mayor parte de la contaminación en el planeta se debe a las industrias.	The majority of the pollution of the planet is due to industries.
Pienso que las centrales nucleares representan un riesgo para todos.	I think that nuclear power plants represent a risk for everyone.

Si todos trabajamos juntos, podremos hacer un cambio.	If we all work together, we will be able to make a change.
La solución es encontrar una fuente alternativa de energía.	The solution is to find an alternative source of energy.
Tengo la intención de comprar más productos orgánicos y productos de comercio justo.	I intend to buy more organic and fair trade products.

Write a sentence to describe an environmental problem using each of the following adjectives.

Remember to make them agree with the noun they are describing.

mundial – worldwide
peligroso – dangerous
dañino – harmful
grave – serious
preocupante – worrying

EXAM TASK

Escribe un blog sobre la importancia de cuidar el medioambiente. Puedes dar más información, pero tienes que incluir:

- lo que haces para ayudar al medioambiente
- la importancia de salvar el planeta
- lo que vas a hacer en casa para ahorrar energía

Aim to write 90–120 words. Try to stick within these limits. There are no extra marks for writing more than this! The second bullet point is asking for your opinions – try to justify them as much as possible. The third bullet point requires you to use the future tense.

SOCIAL ISSUES

¿Cuál es el problema social que te preocupa más?

What is the social problem that worries you the most?

Lo que me preocupa es el problema mundial del desempleo porque la crisis económica ha afectado a tantas personas. Creo que los gobiernos de los países ricos deberían mejorar la situación y crear más puestos de trabajo.

As far as I'm concerned, the biggest problem in the world is unemployment because the economic crisis has affected so many people. I think that the governments of rich countries should improve the situation and create more jobs.

¿Qué se puede hacer para resolver los problemas de la pobreza?

What can we do to solve the problems of poverty?

Me parece que las donaciones a las organizaciones locales o internacionales son sumamente importantes. Aparte de dinero, también se podrían donar alimentos, ropa, muebles, juguetes y libros viejos a los albergues locales.

I think that donations to local or international organisations are extremely important. Apart from money, you could also donate food, clothes, furniture, toys and old books to local hostels.

¿Crees que el gobierno debería ayudar a las personas sin hogar? ¿Por qué (no)?

Do you think the government should help the homeless? Why (not)?

Creo que es esencial combatir el problema de las personas sin hogar y el gobierno tiene la responsabilidad de ayudarles. En mi opinión, el gobierno debería construir más albergues, viviendas sociales y centros de servicios sociales.

I think it's essential to combat the problem of homelessness and the government has a responsibility to help homeless people. In my opinion, the government should build more hostels, social housing and centres for social services.

Describe una cosa que hiciste recientemente para ayudar a los demás.
Describe one thing you have done recently to help other people.

Ayudé a recaudar fondos en el colegio y mis amigos y yo organizamos una venta de pasteles.
Recaudamos más de cien libras y donamos el dinero a una organización benéfica local.
I helped to raise money at school and my friends and I organised a cake sale. We raised more
than a hundred pounds and we donated the money to a local charity.

¿Qué te gustaría hacer para ayudar a los demás?
What would you like to do to help other people?

Después de mis exámenes me gustaría
trabajar como voluntario/a porque creo que
es importante ayudar a mi comunidad local.
Trabajar de voluntario/a es crucial para marcar
una diferencia real y creo que sería una
experiencia gratificante.
After my exams, I would like to work as a
volunteer because I think it's important to help
my local community. Working as a volunteer is
crucial to make a real difference and I think it
would be a rewarding experience.

EXAM TASK

Answer the questions in English.
Promovemos y defendemos los derechos de los
niños en más de 190 países desde hace más de 68
años. La mayor parte de nuestros fondos provienen
de contribuciones de ciudadanos y del sector
privado.

Las primeras horas después de una emergencia
son fundamentales para salvar vidas y garantizar
la protección de los niños. Con tu contribución a
nuestro fondo de emergencias, podemos enviar
recursos de forma inmediata ante cualquier
emergencia o crisis humanitaria. Dona ahora en
línea o haz tu donación por transferencia bancaria.
Ayúdanos a ayudarles.

1. What does the charity do?
2. Where does the majority of their money come
   from?
3. What does the text say about the first few hours
   after an emergency?
4. What will the charity be able to do with your
   donation?
5. How can you donate money?

Read the text once, then read the questions,
then read the text again. Use cognates
(words that are similar to English ones) or
near cognates to help you work out the
meaning of certain words.

How to talk about social issues:

- Say which global issue worries you and use
  appropriate phrases to give your opinions – e.g.
  lo que me preocupa es … (what worries me is …).
  You could explain what kind of problems the issue
  causes or how it affects people, and you could also
  say what you think will happen in the future.
- You need to give several reasons why it's important
  to help other people. You could also mention
  what you have done recently to help others
  – e.g. charity events at school, raising money,
  volunteering. Don't worry if you haven't done any
  of these things – just make it up!
- You can also mention what individuals can
  do – e.g. todo el mundo puede … (everyone
  can …) – or should do – e.g. todo el mundo
  debería … (everyone should …) – and what the
  government should do – e.g. el gobierno debería
  … (the government should …). This is a good
  opportunity to include the subjunctive if you
  can – e.g. es importante que hagamos más para
  ayudar (it's important that we do more to help).

SOCIAL ISSUES

Hay muchos problemas sociales en el mundo y debemos buscar soluciones.	There are many social problems in the world and we must look for solutions.
Una cosa que me preocupa es la pobreza extrema.	One thing that worries me is extreme poverty.
Para mí, lo más importante es ayudar a los demás.	For me, the most important thing is helping other people.
Creo que las organizaciones benéficas hacen un trabajo importantísimo.	I think charities do a really important job.
Desgraciadamente, tengo que reconocer que no hay una solución fácil.	Unfortunately, I have to admit that there isn't an easy solution.
Opino que cada persona en el mundo debería tener las mismas oportunidades.	I'm of the opinion that every person in the world should have the same opportunities.
Solo unidos como humanos podremos erradicar algunos de estos problemas sociales.	Only united as human beings will we be able to eradicate some of these social problems.
En realidad, es un problema de la humanidad entera.	In reality, it's a problem for the whole of humanity.
Es un gran problema a nivel mundial y por desgracia afecta a muchos países.	It's a big problem on a world level and unfortunately it affects many countries.
Lamentablemente, hay muchos países en desarrollo que todavía se enfrentan a graves problemas sociales.	Unfortunately, there are still many developing countries that face serious social problems.
Los países en desarrollo y las personas que viven en ellos necesitan nuestra ayuda y nuestro apoyo.	Developing countries and the people who live in them need our help and support.
En el mundo hay millones de personas que duermen en las calles bajo plásticos o cartones.	In the world there are millions of people who sleep in the streets under plastic bags or boxes.
Me preocupa el hecho de que uno de cada cinco niños no tiene acceso a la educación primaria.	I worry about the fact that one in five children don't have access to primary education.
Considero que la situación más urgente es la salud de los niños.	I consider the most urgent situation to be children's health.
En los últimos diez años, el problema ha aumentado.	In the last ten years, the problem has increased.
No se pueden negar los derechos humanos.	You can't deny human rights.
Muchas personas tienen que huir de la pobreza, injusticia y represión.	Many people have to flee from poverty, injustice and repression.
Me gustaría asistir a una manifestación para protestar contra la discriminación.	I would like to attend a demonstration to protest against discrimination.

Top tips for the conversation:

- Listen carefully to the question. Work out whether the question asked uses the present, past or future tense so that you use the same tense in your answer.
- Speak clearly and loudly.
- Don't worry if you hesitate. Don't use 'umm' or 'err' as we do in English but try to use some Spanish words instead – e.g. bueno ..., pues ... or a ver ...
- Give a reason or an opinion wherever possible – don't just answer yes or no – sí or no. Learn three different ways of expressing 'I think that' or 'in my opinion' in Spanish and try to use them in your answers.
- Say lots! The conversation is your chance to show what you can do.

EXAM TASK

Here are some possible questions to which you can prepare answers. Practise them aloud and work on your accent.

- **¿Crees que es importante ayudar a los demás? ¿Por qué (no)?** Do you think it's important to help other people? Why (not)?
- **¿Cuál es tu organización benéfica preferida? ¿Por qué?** Which charity is your favourite? Why?
- **¿Cómo podemos ayudar a las personas desfavorecidas?** How can we help underprivileged people?
- **¿Qué vas a hacer en el colegio para recaudar fondos?** What are you going to do at school to raise money?
- **Háblame de un evento benéfico al que fuiste.** Talk to me about a charity event you went to.
- **¿Qué se debería hacer para resolver los problemas del mundo?** What should be done to solve the problems in the world?

CURRENT AND FUTURE STUDY AND EMPLOYMENT

CURRENT STUDY

The sub-theme of **Current Study** is divided into two areas. Here are some suggestions of topics to revise:

SCHOOL/COLLEGE LIFE
- school day
- comparison of the school system in different countries
- school facilities
- school trips
- clubs
- rules and regulations
- advantages and disadvantages of school uniform

SCHOOL/COLLEGE STUDIES
- subjects and opinions
- examinations
- workload
- advantages and disadvantages of homework
- study problems
- the importance of education

LISTENING TECHNIQUE

Use your preparation time sensibly – check you understand what you need to do for each question and make a note of any keywords or phrases which may be useful.

Read the questions carefully and make sure you give the required information – e.g. what, why, when, etc. Watch out for negatives. The question 'Which subject does she like?' requires a very different answer to 'Which subject does she **not** like?'

Some of the questions will be in Spanish so make sure you learn the question words carefully. Always answer in the same language as the question.

Check carefully how many marks are available for the question. If you are asked to tick four boxes, make sure you don't tick more than four. You will lose marks if you do.

SCHOOL/COLLEGE LIFE

¿Qué piensas del uniforme escolar?
What do you think of school uniform?

Diría que es práctico y bastante cómodo. Estoy a favor del uniforme porque todos somos iguales y es fácil vestirse por la mañana. Sin embargo, la verdad es que preferiría llevar vaqueros.
I would say that it's practical and quite comfortable. I'm in favour of uniform as we are all equal and it's easy to get dressed in the morning. Nevertheless, the truth is that I would prefer to wear jeans.

¿Qué haces como actividades extraescolares?
What extracurricular activities do you do?

En este momento no hago nada porque tengo demasiados deberes, pero el año pasado hice atletismo. Después de mis exámenes tengo la intención de volver al club de atletismo.
At the moment I don't do anything because I have too much homework, but last year I did athletics. After my exams I intend to go back to the athletics club.

¿Cómo son tus profesores?
What are your teachers like?

Tenemos suerte porque los profesores son muy pacientes y siempre están dispuestos a ayudarnos. No obstante, hay algunos profesores muy estrictos y mi profesora de química grita mucho. ¡Todos pensamos que los profesores nos dan demasiado trabajo!
We are lucky because the teachers are very patient and always ready to help us. However, there are some very strict teachers and my chemistry teacher shouts a lot. We all think that the teachers give us too much work!

¿Qué hiciste en el colegio ayer?
What did you do in school yesterday?

Ayer tuve dos exámenes muy difíciles y fue un día muy largo. ¡No quiero suspender!
Yesterday I had two difficult exams and it was a very long day. I don't want to fail!

¿Cómo sería tu colegio ideal?
What would your ideal school be like?

Mi colegio no es muy grande así que mi colegio ideal tendría más instalaciones deportivas. El deporte es muy importante para mí y me gustaría tener más canchas de tenis y una piscina olímpica. Si yo fuera el/la director/a, construiría un polideportivo para los alumnos.

My school isn't very big so my ideal school would have more sports facilities. Sport is very important to me and I would like more tennis courts and an Olympic-sized pool. If I were the head teacher, I would build a sports centre for the pupils.

GRAMMAR

Talking about your school

To say what you have to do at school you can use the structure **tener que + infinitive** – e.g. **tengo que estudiar** diez asignaturas (I have to study ten subjects).

There are lots of reflexive phrases you can use to talk about school rules:

- se debe + **infinitive** (you must …) – e.g. **se debe llevar** uniforme (you must wear uniform)
- se tiene que + **infinitive** (you have to …) – e.g. **se tiene que respetar** a los demás (you have to respect others)
- (no) se permite + **infinitive** (… is (not) allowed) – e.g. **no se permite llevar** maquillaje (make-up is not allowed)

If you want to say what you should do, then you will need to use **se debe** in the conditional:

- se debería + **infinitive** (you should …) – e.g. **se debería estudiar** muy duro (you should study very hard)

Other expressions for talking about school rules include:

- es necesario + **infinitive** (it's necessary …) – e.g. **es necesario hacer** los deberes (it's necessary to do homework)
- no está permitido/está prohibido + **infinitive** (… is not allowed) – e.g. **no está permitido llevar** joyas (wearing jewellery is not allowed)
- hay que + **infinitive** (you have to …) – e.g. **hay que trabajar** duro (you have to work hard)

EXAM TASK

Read this literary text and answer the questions in English.

En general, cuando el profesor le quita un objeto a un alumno por no prestar atención a la clase, se lo devuelve al tocar el timbre del recreo. En el colegio de Hernán las reglas eran diferentes, existía una ley que decía que todos los objetos quitados por los profesores en horario de clase debían ser depositados en el cuarto '15/60'. Este cuarto estaba ubicado en la planta baja, junto a la sala de profesores. Los profesores estaban obligados a pasar los objetos al director y, al final del día, el director los llevaba al cuarto '15/60'.

Most of the verbs in this extract are in the imperfect tense.

1. Why would a teacher usually take something away from a pupil?
2. When would the pupil usually expect to get it back?
3. What is different about Hernán's school?
4. Where is room '15/60'?
5. What happens if a teacher confiscates something from a pupil?

Questions on literary texts may be longer and require more thought than the questions at the start of your paper, so make sure you leave enough time to answer them.

SCHOOL/COLLEGE LIFE

No me gusta la mañana porque las clases comienzan temprano y tenemos más de tres horas de clases.

I don't like the morning because lessons start early and we have more than three hours of lessons.

Mi colegio no ofrece ningún tipo de club después de las clases.

My school doesn't offer any type of club after lessons.

Tenemos mucha suerte porque el colegio ofrece muchas actividades extraescolares.

We are very lucky because the school offers many extracurricular activities.

No soy miembro de un club extraescolar porque me gusta tener la tarde libre todos los días.

I'm not a member of an extracurricular club because I like to have the afternoon free every day.

Normalmente durante el recreo hablo con mis amigos, pero a veces voy a la biblioteca para hacer mis deberes.

Usually during break I talk to my friends, but sometimes I go to the library to do my homework.

Paso dos horas en el patio charlando con mis amigos durante el día.

I spend two hours in the yard chatting with my friends during the day.

Me encantaba mi colegio de primaria porque no era estricto y los maestros eran muy pacientes con los alumnos.

I loved my primary school because it wasn't strict and the teachers wery very patient with the pupils.

El trabajo era fácil y no había deberes ni exámenes.

The work was easy and there wasn't any homework or exams.

Opino que los profesores son muy negativos y también nos dan mucho trabajo en clase.

I think that the teachers are very negative and they also give us lots of work in class.

La cantina vende comida bastante barata pero no es muy buena.

The canteen sells quite cheap food but it isn't very good.

Prefiero traer bocadillos porque siempre hay colas en la cantina.

I prefer to bring sandwiches because there are always queues in the canteen.

Algunos alumnos son muy habladores en clase y se comportan mal.

Some pupils are very talkative in class and behave badly.

El problema del acoso escolar afecta a muchos estudiantes.

The problem of school bullying affects lots of students.

Creo que los edificios son bastante feos, algunos son modernos pero las instalaciones son antiguas.

I think the buildings are quite ugly, some are modern but the facilities are old.

En mi colegio hay más o menos mil estudiantes de entre once y dieciocho años.

In my school there are around a thousand students between eleven and eighteen years old.

Mi colegio anterior era más pequeño, pero más moderno.

My previous school was smaller, but it was more modern.

Tengo que llevar uniforme escolar y no me gusta nada porque es muy incómodo.	I have to wear school uniform and I don't like it because it's very uncomfortable.
En mi opinión, el uniforme escolar evita problemas de discriminación y promociona la igualdad.	In my opinion, school uniform avoids problems with discipline and promotes equality.
Encuentro las reglas muy estrictas, pero entiendo la importancia de la disciplina.	I find the rules very strict, but I understand the importance of discipline.
Mi colegio ideal sería moderno y grande y tendría buenas instalaciones.	My ideal school would be modern and big and it would have good facilities.
Si yo fuera el director/a, eliminaría muchas reglas y aboliría los deberes.	If I were the head teacher, I would eliminate many rules and I would abolish homework.

You may be asked to describe your school day in your speaking or writing exam. Look at this description:

El colegio empieza a las nueve y termina a las tres. Hay cinco clases cada día y cada clase dura una hora. Hay un recreo a las once y la hora de comer es a la una.

Try not to give answers like this all the time. This is correct Spanish but it's just a list! There are no opinions, no justifications, no reasons and it's all in one tense. This would be a much better answer:

El colegio empieza a las nueve y termina a las tres. En mi opinión, es un día muy largo. Hay cinco clases cada día y cada clase dura una hora. Ayer tuve dos clases de matemáticas, ¡que aburrido! Hay un recreo a las once y la hora de comer es a la una. Durante el recreo me encanta jugar al fútbol con mis amigos.

EXAM TASK

Remember:

In your role play you will have to use the present tense as well as at least one other tense. Watch out for 'trigger' words which show you which tense to use – e.g. **ayer** (yesterday) and **el fin de semana pasado** (last weekend) show you need to use the preterite tense, and **mañana** (tomorrow) and **la semana que viene** (next week) show you need to use the future tense.

If there are no trigger words – as in the first two bullet points that follow – then you will need to use the present tense. Remember that you don't need to give any extra information but you will need to answer using full sentences, not single words or short phrases.

Here are some examples of possible role play prompts on this topic:

- Tu colegio (**dos** detalles)
- Tu uniforme escolar (opinión)
- El recreo – ayer
- Los deberes – el fin de semana pasado
- Después del colegio – mañana
- Las actividades extraescolares – la semana que viene

SCHOOL/COLLEGE STUDIES

¿Cuál es tu asignatura preferida? ¿Por qué?

What is your favourite subject? Why?

Mi asignatura preferida en este momento es la historia porque el trabajo es fascinante y el profesor es gracioso. También, mis amigos están en la misma clase y tenemos suerte porque el profesor no nos da demasiados deberes.

My favourite subject at the moment is history as the work is fascinating and the teacher is funny. Also, my friends are in the same class and we are lucky because the teacher doesn't give us too much homework.

¿Piensas que los exámenes son importantes?

Do you think exams are important?

Según mis padres y mis profesores, los exámenes son esenciales para tener éxito en la vida. Estoy un poco obsesionado/a con mis notas y no sé que haré si suspendo.

According to my parents and my teachers, exams are essential in order to succeed in life. I'm a bit obsessed by my grades and I don't know what I will do if I fail.

¿Hay demasiada presión en el colegio?

Is there too much pressure at school?

Claro que sí, estoy muy estresado/a este año. El trabajo es mucho más difícil ya que tenemos exámenes y tengo que pasar todos mis ratos libres estudiando. Mis profesores son muy exigentes y hay mucha presión.

Yes of course – I am very stressed this year. The work is much harder because we have exams and I have to spend all my free time studying. My teachers are very demanding and there is a lot of pressure.

¿Qué deberes hiciste el fin de semana pasado?

What homework did you do last weekend?

Pasé el fin de semana entero trabajando porque tenía tantos deberes. Lo pasé muy mal. El fin de semana que viene no voy a hacer nada.

I spent the whole weekend working because I had so much homework. I had a really bad time. Next weekend I'm not going to do anything.

¿Qué vas a estudiar el año que viene?
What are you going to study next year?

La verdad es que no sé qué quiero hacer. Por una parte, me gustaría hacer algo relacionado con los idiomas, pero al mismo tiempo no sé si debería elegir ciencia y tecnología. Lo más importante es sacar buenas notas.
The truth is that I don't know what I want to do. On the one hand, I'd like to do something to do with languages, but at the same time I don't know if I should choose science and technology. The most important thing is getting good grades.

You can use these time phrases to talk about how often you do something at school:

a veces/de vez en cuando – sometimes
frecuentemente/a menudo – often
normalmente – usually
siempre – always
raramente/rara vez – rarely
nunca – never
cada jueves – every Thursday
cada semana – every week
todos los días/cada día – every day
después del colegio/de las clases – after school/
    lessons
por la mañana/tarde – in the morning/afternoon

EXAM TASK

Answer the questions in English.

En un mundo global es cada vez más importante aprender más de un idioma. Te ayudará a mejorar tu carrera profesional pero también a hablar con personas de otros países y disfrutar más tus viajes. Además, según algunos estudios, la gente bilingüe es más feliz y más rica.

Una vez que aprendes una segunda lengua, te será más fácil aprender otras. Finalmente, aprender otro idioma ayuda a las personas a entender que el mundo no es todo igual y que existen diversidades culturales y las prepara para el futuro.

1. What reasons are there for learning more than one language according to the first paragraph? Give **two** details.
2. What does the article claim about bilingual people?
3. Once you've learned one language, what becomes easier?
4. What is the final benefit of learning a language that is mentioned?

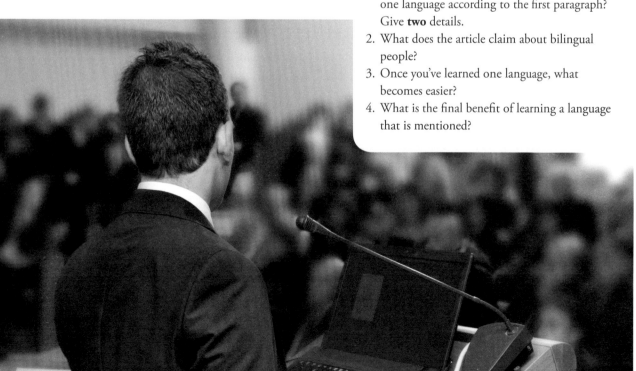

SCHOOL/COLLEGE STUDIES

Este año voy a terminar la enseñanza obligatoria y no sé qué voy a hacer en septiembre.	This year I'm going to finish compulsory education and I don't know what I'm going to do in September.
Lo positivo de mi colegio es que hay una amplia gama de asignaturas.	The positive thing about my school is that there is a wide range of subjects.
Me preocupan mucho las exigencias de mis padres y los fracasos académicos.	I'm very worried about my parents' demands and about academic failures.
Creo que sufro de estrés académico a causa de los exámenes.	I think I suffer from stress at school because of the exams.
Estoy muy ansioso/a porque tengo muchos deberes y los encuentro muy difíciles.	I'm very anxious because I have a lot of homework and I find it very difficult.
No soy una persona muy trabajadora y no saco muy buenas notas.	I am not a very hard-working person and I don't get very good grades.
No soy una persona muy creativa y prefiero la lógica, entonces las matemáticas me resultan muy fáciles.	I'm not a very creative person and I prefer logic, so maths is easy for me.
Me encanta el inglés porque tengo buena imaginación y me encanta escribir ensayos.	I love English because I have a good imagination and I love writing essays.
Lo que realmente me gusta es debatir los problemas mundiales en clase.	What I really like is debating world problems in class.
Tengo problemas con mis compañeros de clase y sufro acoso escolar de vez en cuando.	I have problems with my classmates and I suffer bullying from time to time.
Por desgracia, el estrés es parte de la vida de un estudiante.	Unfortunately, stress is part of the life of a student.
Prefiero las asignaturas científicas porque me encanta analizar y experimentar.	I prefer scientific subjects because I love analysing and experimenting.
No me gusta nada esta asignatura porque creo que es muy aburrida y no es útil para mi futuro.	I don't like that subject because I think that it's very boring and it isn't useful for my future.
El dibujo no es mi especialidad y no tengo ningún talento artístico.	Art isn't my speciality and I don't have any artistic talent.
Me apasiona todo lo relacionado con la historia porque me fascina aprender sobre las generaciones anteriores.	I love everything to do with history because I am fascinated by learning about previous generations.

Las ciencias me cuestan mucho y tengo que trabajar muy duro en clase.	Science is very tough for me and I have to work very hard in class.
Si trabajo duro, aprobaré mis exámenes.	If I work hard, I will pass my exams.
Los profesores han dicho que tenemos que estudiar mucho este año.	The teachers have said that we have to study a lot this year.

Remember that you will be marked for accuracy at both Foundation and Higher level. Carefully check spellings, accents, genders, plurals and tenses.

Remember to include additional tenses, if possible, to show off your grammatical knowledge. In the task below, for example, you are asked to write about your primary school (past tense) and your plans for September (future tense). Why not try to talk about your ideal school or what you would like to do in the future as well (conditional tense)?

As with the conversation part of the speaking exam, this is your opportunity to show what you can do. If you're not quite sure how to express something, write it another way – it doesn't have to be true as long as it makes sense!

EXAM TASK

Escribe un artículo para la revista de tu colegio. Puedes dar más información, pero tienes que incluir:

- tu escuela primaria (en el pasado)
- tu colegio (en el presente)
- lo que vas a estudiar el año que viene

You are in control in this exam but don't just write what you want – make sure you answer the question. Try to spend equal time and attention on all three bullet points. Aim to write 90–120 words in total. Here are some key verbs in the yo form to help you:

	Imperfect	Preterite	Present	Immediate future	Future	Conditional
ir – to go	iba	fui	voy	voy a ir	iré	iría
hacer – to make/do	hacía	hice	hago	voy a hacer	haré	haría
tener – to have	tenía	tuve	tengo	voy a tener	tendré	tendría
estudiar – to study	estudiaba	estudié	estudio	voy a estudiar	estudiaré	estudiaría

CURRENT AND FUTURE STUDY AND EMPLOYMENT

WORLD OF WORK

The sub-theme of **World of Work** is divided into two areas. Here are some suggestions of topics to revise:

WORK EXPERIENCE AND PART-TIME JOBS

- advantages and disadvantages of work experience
- saving money
- pocket money
- voluntary work
- part-time jobs
- how you spend the money you earn

SKILLS AND PERSONAL QUALITIES

- personality traits
- personal skills
- skills required for different jobs
- application letters
- job interviews

READING TECHNIQUE

You can expect to see a range of texts of different lengths, written in formal and informal styles and for a variety of audiences – e.g. magazine articles, information leaflets, adverts, literary texts, etc.

Read the question carefully and scan through the text for any keywords related to the question. Check the question again to make sure you have a clear idea of what exactly is being asked.

Don't leave any questions unanswered – try to rule out any options that you are sure are wrong before making a sensible guess.

WORK EXPERIENCE AND PART-TIME JOBS

¿Qué haces para ganar dinero?
What do you do to earn money?

Antes, trabajaba en una tienda los fines de semana, pero ahora tengo demasiado trabajo escolar. Tengo suerte porque mis padres me dan diez libras cada semana si ayudo con las tareas domésticas.
Before, I used to work in a shop at the weekend but now I have too much schoolwork. I am lucky because my parents give me ten pounds every week if I help with household chores.

¿Es importante trabajar durante las vacaciones escolares?
Is it important to work during the school holidays?

En general, creo es una buena idea trabajar durante las vacaciones. La primera ventaja obvia es ganar dinero, pero también ofrece la oportunidad de aprender nuevas cosas y reforzar el currículo.
In general, I think it's a good idea to work during the holidays. The first obvious advantage is earning money, but it also offers the opportunity to learn new things and strengthen your CV.

¿Cuáles son los aspectos negativos de un trabajo a tiempo parcial?
What are the negative aspects of a part-time job?

Mis amigos me dicen que sus trabajos no están bien pagados. El trabajo puede ser monótono y pienso que es muy difícil combinar los estudios y el trabajo.
My friends tell me that their jobs are not well paid. The work can be monotonous and I think it's very difficult to combine studies and work.

¿Qué te gustaría hacer como trabajo de verano?
What would you like to do as a summer job?

Me gustaría trabajar al aire libre como socorrista. Sería un trabajo bastante variado y tendría la oportunidad de ayudar a la gente.
I would like to work outdoors as a lifeguard. It would be quite a varied job and I would have the opportunity to help people.

¿Has hecho prácticas laborales?
Have you done work experience?

Tengo que admitir que nunca he trabajado. Tampoco he tenido la oportunidad de hacer prácticas laborales. Un día me gustaría ser periodista, por eso debería hacer prácticas en la oficina del periódico regional.

I have to admit I have never worked. Neither have I had the opportunity to do work experience. One day I would like to be a journalist, so I should do a work placement in the office of the regional newspaper.

Multiple-choice questions

You are likely to have at least one multiple-choice question in your reading and/or listening exam. The question may be in English or Spanish or use pictures. Top tips:

- Don't answer too soon! Make sure you read all of the options before choosing your answer, and don't just stop when you come to the one that seems most likely.
- Some of the answers may be deliberately trying to trick you! Several alternatives may seem correct, so it is important to read the text and the questions carefully.
- If you are not sure of an answer, guess ... but do so methodically. Eliminate some choices you know are wrong. Try to narrow down the answer to one or two alternatives and then compare them. Finally, make an informed decision.

EXAM TASK

Now practise your multiple-choice strategies on this task.

Miles de jóvenes, muchos acompañados por sus padres, acudieron hoy al Departamento del Trabajo para solicitar empleos de verano. Muchos de los interesados llegaron desde las ocho de la mañana para hacer cola, pero las puertas del centro solo abrieron a las diez de la mañana.

Hay mil empleos disponibles, el empleo es solo por el mes de junio y los jóvenes deberán entregar sus solicitudes durante los días del 30 abril al 4 de mayo.

1. ¿Qué buscan los jóvenes?
   a. trabajos a tiempo parcial
   b. trabajos de verano
   c. el Departamento de Trabajo
2. ¿A que hora abrió el Departamento?
   a. 8.00
   b. 20.00
   c. 10.00
3. ¿Cuántos puestos hay?
   a. 1000
   b. 30
   c. 20
4. ¿Cuánto tiempo dura el puesto?
   a. el mes de mayo
   b. el mes de abril
   c. el mes de junio

WORK EXPERIENCE AND PART-TIME JOBS

No tengo un trabajo en este momento ya que voy al colegio.	I don't have a job at the moment as I go to school.
Mis padres no me permiten trabajar porque piensan que mis estudios son demasiado importantes.	My parents won't let me work as they think my studies are too important.
No tengo empleo a tiempo parcial porque no hay puestos disponibles para los jóvenes.	I don't have a part-time job because there are no posts available for young people.
Si tuviera la oportunidad, me gustaría encontrar un trabajo de verano para tener más dinero para gastar.	If I had the opportunity, I would like to find a summer job to have more money to spend.
El año que viene espero encontrar un trabajo de verano.	Next year I hope to find a summer job.
Si encuentro un trabajo a tiempo parcial, ahorraré mi dinero para comprar ropa.	If I find a part-time job, I will save my money to buy clothes.
Este verano pasaré quince días trabajando en la oficina de mi tío.	This summer I will spend a fortnight working in my uncle's office.
Gasto la mayoría de mi dinero, pero trato de ahorrar cinco libras a la semana.	I spend most of my money, but I try to save five pounds a week.
En mi opinión, es esencial trabajar y ganar dinero.	In my opinion, it's essential to work and earn money.
El trabajo es duro y mi jefe es muy exigente.	The work is hard and my boss is very demanding.
Preferiría trabajar como dependiente porque ganaría más dinero.	I would prefer to work as a sales assistant because I would earn more money.
Es una buena experiencia para el futuro y sería bueno para mi currículo.	It is good experience for the future and it would be good for my CV.
Este verano trabajaré en un supermercado los fines de semana.	This summer I will work in a supermarket at the weekend.
Trabajaba cinco horas por semana, pero me resultaba imposible estudiar y trabajar al mismo tiempo.	I used to work five hours a week, but it was impossible for me to study and work at the same time.
Limpiaba la casa de mi vecino una vez a la semana, pero ahora no tengo suficiente tiempo.	I used to clean my neighbour's house once a week, but now I don't have enough time.
Espero poder hacer unas prácticas que me faciliten el acceso al mercado laboral.	I hope to be able to do some work experience that will give me ease of access to the job market.

He hecho dos periodos de prácticas y me sirvieron para reafirmarme en mi vocación.	I've done two periods of work experience and they served to reaffirm my vocation.
Los días pasaron muy rápidamente y fue una experiencia educativa porque aprendí un montón de nuevas habilidades.	The days passed very quickly and it was an educational experience because I learned loads of new skills.
Si hiciera mis prácticas otra vez, sería más paciente con los clientes.	If I did my work experience again, I would be more patient with the clients.

Useful phrases for describing a picture:

en esta foto veo … – in this photo I see …
el foco principal de la foto es … – the main focus of the photo is …
la foto trata de … – the photo is about …
en la foto hay … – in the photo there is …
en primer plano – in the foreground
al fondo – in the background
a la derecha/izquierda – on the right/left

Expressing opinions:

creo que/pienso que/opino que/me parece que – I think that
en mi opinión – in my opinion
me da la impresión de que – I get the impression that
me parece que – it seems that
desde mi punto de vista – from my point of view
por mi parte – as for me
a mi parecer – in my mind

EXAM TASK

Answer these questions in Spanish.

- **Describe la foto.** (Foundation)/**¿De qué trata esta foto?** (Higher) Describe the photo./What is happening in the photo?
- **¿Es importante ganar dinero? ¿Por qué (no)?** Is it important to earn money? Why (not)?
- **Los jóvenes necesitan experiencia laboral. ¿Qué piensas?** Young people need experience of the world of work. What do you think?
- **¿Te gustaría encontrar un trabajo a tiempo parcial?** Would you like a part-time job?

SKILLS AND PERSONAL QUALITIES

¿Cuáles son tus cualidades personales?
What are your personal qualities?

Me relaciono con la gente con facilidad. Creo que soy una persona bastante extrovertida porque no me resulta difícil expresar mis opiniones y hacer preguntas.
I relate easily to other people. I consider myself to be quite an extrovert because I don't find it difficult to express my opinions and ask questions.

¿Cuáles son tus habilidades para el mercado laboral?
What skills do you have for the world of work?

Soy organizado/a, eficiente y práctico/a, y me enorgullezco de hacer el trabajo lo mejor posible. También tengo una habilidad para motivar a los demás y no me da miedo hablar en público.
I am organised, efficient and practical, and I am proud of doing the best work possible. I also have an ability to motivate others and I'm not afraid of speaking in public.

¿Cuáles son las habilidades esenciales para encontrar un buen trabajo?
What are the essential skills for finding a good job?

Primero, es importante hablar una lengua extranjera. Para tener éxito, hay que aprender de los errores e intentar resolver los problemas. Además, se debería proyectar una actitud positiva y mostrar entusiasmo.
Firstly, it's important to speak a foreign language. To be successful, you have to learn from mistakes and try to resolve problems. Furthermore, you should project a positive attitude and show enthusiasm.

¿Cómo sería tu jefe ideal?
What would your ideal boss be like?

Mi jefe ideal tendría que ser un mentor y escucharía a los demás. Sería exigente, pero al mismo tiempo amable. Un buen jefe tiene que motivar a los empleados y valorar su trabajo.
My ideal boss would have to be a mentor and would listen to others. They would be demanding but friendly at the same time. A good boss has to motivate employees and value their work.

¿Cuál ha sido tu mayor éxito en el colegio?
What has been your biggest success at school?

Mi mayor éxito escolar ha sido aprobar todos mis exámenes el año pasado. Tuve que trabajar muy duro durante el año, pero al final saque muy buenas notas.
My biggest success at school has been passing all my exams last year. I had to work very hard during the whole year, but in the end I got very good grades.

When you are talking about your skills and personal qualities you will often need to give examples to illustrate the points you are making. Here are some useful expressions in Spanish to link and extend your sentences:

por ejemplo – for example
como – like
tal/tales como – such as
es decir – that's to say
en cuanto a/respecto a – regarding, with regards to
es evidente que – it is obvious that
específicamente – specifically
porque – because
a causa de – because of
cuando – when
puesto que/ya que – since
pero – but

Match 1–10 to a–j.

1. Actitud positiva hacia el trabajo y la vida
2. Facilidad para la comunicación
3. Capacidad para relacionarse con los demás
4. Confianza en sí mismo
5. Capacidad de análisis y resolución de problemas
6. Adaptabilidad
7. Automotivación
8. Liderazgo
9. Trabajo en equipo
10. Conocimientos en el área específica

a. Self-motivation
b. Ability to analyse and resolve problems
c. Team working
d. Positive attitude towards work and life
e. Specific knowledge
f. Adaptability
g. Ability to communicate
h. Leadership
i. Ability to get on well with others
j. Self-confidence

SKILLS AND PERSONAL QUALITIES

Mis profesores dicen que soy cooperativo/a y constante.	My teachers say I am cooperative and persistent.
Era tímido/a cuando era más joven pero ahora tengo más autoconfianza.	I was shy when I was younger but now I have more self-confidence.
Siempre escucho a los demás y tengo en cuenta sus opiniones.	I always listen to others and take their opinions into account.
Hablo y expreso mis ideas bien delante de otras personas.	I speak and express my ideas well in front of other people.
Me gustaría ser más adaptable y flexible.	I would like to be more adaptable and flexible.
Soy capaz de utilizar la tecnología de forma eficiente.	I'm capable of using technology efficiently.
Si fuera más responsable, tendría más capacidad de liderazgo.	If I were more responsible, I would have more leadership ability.
Lo más importante es crear una buena primera impresión.	The most important thing is to make a good first impression.
Creo que lo más esencial en la vida es poder comunicarse con los demás.	I think the most essential thing in life is being able to communicate with others.
Mi mayor fortaleza es mi habilidad para mantenerme centrado en mi trabajo.	My biggest strength is my ability to remain focused on my work.
Diría que la creatividad es mi mejor atributo.	I would say creativity is my best attribute.
Mi capacidad para trabajar en equipo ha sido siempre mi fuerte.	My ability to work in a team has always been my strength.
Una de mis debilidades es que suelo ser un poco desorganizado/a.	One of my weaknesses is that I am usually a bit disorganised.
En cuanto a mis defectos, tengo que admitir que me estreso rápidamente.	As far as my defects are concerned, I have to admit that I get stressed quickly.
Intentaré cambiar los rasgos que me molestan.	I will try to change the traits that annoy me.
Lo más importante para mí es el reto de iniciar proyectos porque me encanta asumir riesgos.	The most important thing for me is the challenge of setting up projects because I love taking risks.
Prefiero liderar grupos y tomar muchas decisiones.	I prefer to lead groups and make a lot of decisions.
En cuanto a mis fortalezas, aprendo con facilidad y siempre pienso antes de actuar.	As far as my strengths are concerned, I learn easily and I always think before acting.
Siempre he sido muy ambicioso/a.	I have always been very ambitious.

You can make an ordinary sentence much more impressive by using a variety of sequencers and connectives.

Here are some helpful expressions to improve the quality of your answers – try to vary your Spanish as much as possible:

primero – first
primeramente – firstly
en primer lugar – in the first place
en otras palabras/dicho de otra manera/dicho de otro modo – in other words
por último/finalmente/por fin – finally
en cambio/por otro lado/por otra parte – on the other hand
de hecho/en realidad/en efecto/efectivamente – in fact
no obstante/sin embargo – nevertheless
por lo tanto/por consiguiente/por eso – therefore
por desgracia/desgraciadamente – unfortunately

EXAM TASK

Escribe una frase completa para cada trabajo:

- dentista
- profesor/a
- cocinero/a
- asistente social
- dependiente
- programador/a

Look at the exam task on page 95. Try to use some of the vocabulary to help you here.

CURRENT AND FUTURE STUDY AND EMPLOYMENT

JOBS AND FUTURE PLANS

The sub-theme of **Jobs and Future Plans** is divided into two areas. Here are some suggestions of topics to revise:

APPLYING FOR WORK/STUDY

- job applications
- formal letters
- CVs
- interviews – e.g. for work, college, university
- job adverts

CAREER PLANS

- training and study options
- job opportunities
- working abroad
- future plans
- interviews at an employment agency

WRITING TECHNIQUE

Check how many marks are available for each question so you know how to divide your time in the examination. See how many words you are recommended to write. Make a plan before you start writing.

Always leave time to check your work. Make sure you have:

- been consistent with spellings
- used the correct gender for nouns
- used tenses appropriately
- used the correct endings for verbs
- included a range of sentence structures and vocabulary
- included a range of opinions and justifications

APPLYING FOR WORK/STUDY

¿Quieres continuar con tus estudios el año que viene? ¿Por qué (no)?
Do you want to continue with your studies next year? Why (not)?

La verdad es que la vida escolar me estresa mucho, pero tengo la intención de encontrar un buen trabajo en el futuro entonces tendré que continuar con mis estudios. Voy a estudiar inglés, historia y francés.
In my opinion, school life is stressful but I intend to find a good job in the future, so I will continue with my studies next year. I am going to study English, history and French.

¿Te gustaría ir a la universidad? ¿Por qué (no)?
Would you like to go to university? Why (not)?

Cuando era pequeño/a, mi sueño era ir a la universidad para hacerme abogado/a, pero he cambiado de opinión. Creo que la formación sería demasiado larga y aburrida y también sería muy cara.
When I was younger, my dream was to go to university to become a lawyer, but I have changed my mind. I think that the training would be too long and boring and it would be too expensive.

¿Es esencial para los jóvenes ir a la universidad?
Is it essential for young people to go to university?

Por supuesto, los títulos pueden ayudarnos en el mercado laboral, pero hay otras formas de tener éxito en el mundo. Para tener una vida exitosa hay que ser una persona ambiciosa y trabajadora.
Of course degrees can help us in the job market, but there are other ways to succeed in the world. To have a successful life, you need to be hard-working and ambitious.

¿Cuáles son las ventajas de un año sabático?
What are the advantages of a gap year?

Pienso que un año sabático puede enriquecer la vida. Por ejemplo, se puede aprender una nueva lengua o explorar el mundo.
I think a gap year can enrich life. For example, you could learn a new language or explore the world.

¿Crees que la universidad es demasiado cara? ¿Por qué (no)?
Do you think university is too expensive? Why (not)?

Es verdad que estudiar es cada vez más caro, y tengo que admitir que no sé si vale la pena. Mis padres quieren que vaya a la universidad, pero personalmente preferiría encontrar un buen trabajo.
It's true that studying is becoming more and more expensive, and I have to admit that I don't know if it's worth it. My parents want me to go to university, but personally I would prefer to find a good job.

In this unit, it will be helpful if you can understand and use persuasive language and you will also need to ask questions.
Learn and use the following phrases and remember to vary your Spanish.

To express hope:
> Espero ... – I hope ...
> Tengo el deseo de ... – I have the desire to ...
> Tengo ganas de ... – I am keen to ...

To seek/give information:
> ¿Podría explicar ...? – Could you explain ...?
> (formal)
> ¿Podría decirme ...? – Could you tell me ...?
> (formal)
> ¿Sería posible ...? – Would it be possible ...?

To express intention:
> Tengo la intención de ... – I intend to ...
> Mi objetivo (personal) es ... – My (personal)
> objective is ...

To express interest:
> Estoy particularmente interesado/a en ... – I am
> particularly interested in ...
> Me entusiasma(n) ... – I am enthusiastic about ...
> Me apasiona(n) ... – I am passionate about ...
> Me fascina(n) ... – I am fascinated by ...

EXAM TASK

Translate the following sentences into English:

1. No tengo la intención de ir a la universidad, porque es demasiado cara.
2. Voy a dejar el colegio después de mis exámenes porque preferiría ganar mucho dinero.
3. Tuve una entrevista ayer por la tarde y estaba bastante nervioso.
4. Estoy dispuesto a estudiar duro y espero sacar buenas notas.
5. Los negocios siempre me han interesado y mi objetivo es trabajar en una empresa muy grande.

Watch out for quantifiers and intensifiers – e.g. **demasiado**, **mucho**, **bastante**, **muy**, etc. – and make sure you translate them. You will lose marks if you miss out words.

APPLYING FOR WORK/STUDY

Si no apruebo mis exámenes, haré un aprendizaje.	If I don't pass my exams, I will do an apprenticeship.
A corto plazo, quiero terminar mis estudios para ingresar en la universidad.	In the short term, I want to finish my studies in order to get into university.
Me gustaría ir a un nuevo instituto el año que viene para aprender cosas nuevas.	I would like to go to a new school next year to learn new things.
Continuar con mis estudios me aportará experiencias inolvidables.	Continuing with my studies will give me unforgettable experiences.
Tengo varios objetivos para los próximos años.	I have various objectives for the next few years.
Mis padres me obligaron a continuar con mis estudios.	My parents forced me to continue with my studies.
Estudiar en un nuevo instituto me plantearía numerosos retos.	Studying in a new school would offer me many challenges.
Mis profesores me ayudarán a obtener buenas cualificaciones.	My teachers will help me to get good qualifications.
No quiero ir a la universidad, porque es demasiado cara.	I don't want to go to university, because it's too expensive.
Voy a dejar el colegio después de mis exámenes porque me gustaría ganar dinero.	I'm going to leave school after my exams because I would like to earn money.
Si voy a la universidad, tendré mejores oportunidades laborales en el futuro.	If I go to university, I will have better job opportunities in the future.
Mi instituto tiene una buena reputación y me ofrecerá la oportunidad de prepararme para la universidad.	My school has a good reputation and will offer me the opportunity to prepare for university.
Estoy dispuesto/a a estudiar duro y espero sacar buenas notas.	I am prepared to work hard and I hope to get good grades.
Siempre me ha interesado le tecnología, por eso estudiaré informática el año que viene.	I have always been interested in technology, so I will study ICT next year.
Desde joven he querido estudiar idiomas porque voy a vivir en el extranjero en el futuro.	From a young age I have wanted to study languages because I am going to live abroad in the future.
Tengo la intención de ir a la universidad, pero no quiero vivir lejos.	I intend to go to university, but I don't want to live far away.

Mis padres dicen que los estudios son muy importantes.	My parents say that studies are very important.
Siempre he querido ampliar mis horizontes.	I have always wanted to broaden my horizons.
He aprendido innumerables cosas a través del colegio.	I have learned no end of things at school.
Preferiría hacer un curso de formación profesional.	I would prefer to do a vocational course.
Estoy harto/a de estudiar, por eso voy a solicitar un trabajo que ofrece formación.	I am fed up of studying, so I am going to apply for a job that offers training.

Don't worry if you don't understand the question at first. You won't lose marks if you ask your teacher to repeat what they said.
Here are some useful phrases in Spanish:

> No entiendo/no comprendo – I don't understand
> Todavía no entiendo/no comprendo – I still don't understand
> ¿Puedes repetir (lo), por favor? – Can you please repeat (it)?
> ¿Puedes repetir la pregunta? – Can you repeat the question?
> ¿Qué quiere decir? – What does that mean?
> Perdón – Sorry/pardon
> Lo siento – I'm sorry

EXAM TASK

Here are some examples of conversation questions:

- ¿Cuáles son tus planes para el año que viene? What are your plans for next year?
- ¿Qué te gustaría estudiar en la universidad? What would you like to study at university?
- ¿Qué haces para contribuir a la vida escolar? What do you do to contribute to school life?
- ¿Por qué elegiste tus asignaturas? Why did you choose your subjects?
- ¿Crees que el instituto prepara a los jóvenes para el futuro? Do you think school prepares young people for the future?
- ¿Cuáles son las ventajas de cambiar de instituto después de los exámenes? What are the advantages of changing schools after your exams?

CAREER PLANS

¿Qué quieres hacer más tarde en la vida?
What do you want to do later in life?

> Si apruebo mis exámenes, iré a la universidad, pero no sé que voy a estudiar. Después de terminar mis estudios, espero encontrar un trabajo interesante y bien pagado.
> If I pass my exams, I will go to university, but I don't know what I'm going to study. After my studies, I would like to find an interesting and well-paid job.

¿Es difícil para los jóvenes encontrar un buen trabajo? ¿Por qué (no)?
Is it hard for young people to find a good job? Why (not)?

> No sé por qué es tan difícil encontrar un trabajo hoy en día. Hay mucho desempleo e imagino que no hay suficientes trabajos para los jóvenes que no tienen experiencia.
> I don't know why it's so hard to find a job these days. There is lots of unemployment and I imagine there are not enough jobs for young people who don't have experience.

¿Te gustaría trabajar en el extranjero en el futuro? ¿Por qué (no)?
Would you like to work abroad in the future? Why (not)?

> Para mí, trabajar en el extranjero es una buena idea porque se pueden desarrollar nuevas habilidades. Personalmente, me encantaría trabajar en los Estados Unidos porque allí hay muchas oportunidades.
> In my opinion, working abroad is a good idea because you can develop new skills. Personally, I would like to work in the United States because there are lots of opportunities there.

¿Cómo será tu vida en diez años?
What will your life be like in ten years?

> ¡Espero ser rico/a y feliz! Habré terminado mis estudios y tendré un trabajo gratificante. Viviré en una casa enorme con una piscina y me gustaría casarme y tener hijos.
> I hope to be rich and happy! I will have finished my studies and I will have a rewarding job. I will live in a big house with a swimming pool and I would like to get married and have children.

¿Qué querías hacer cuando eras pequeño/a?
What did you want to do when you were younger?

En el pasado, siempre soñaba con ser cantante porque quería ser famoso/a. Ahora no tengo ningún deseo de ser famoso/a, ¡no me interesa nada!
In the past I always dreamed of being a singer because I wanted to be famous. Now I don't have any desire to be famous – it doesn't interest me at all!

Using the past to talk about future plans

Even when you are talking about your future plans, you may also need to talk about the past for comparison – e.g. **En el pasado quería ir a la universidad, pero ahora prefiero la idea de buscar un trabajo.** (In the past I wanted to go to university but now I prefer the idea of looking for a job.)

Here are some useful phrases in the imperfect tense:

en el pasado, tenía ganas de ... – in the past I wanted to …

hace unos años, tenía la intención de ... – a few years ago I intended to …

cuando era más joven, mi trabajo ideal era ... – when I was younger my ideal job was …

siempre esperaba/quería ... – I always hoped/ wanted …

Future plans

Although you can discuss upcoming events and plans using the future tense, remember that you can also use the immediate future by using **ir a + infinitive** – e.g. **voy a estudiar** historia (I am going to study history). You can also use the following constructions to talk about the future:

* **querer + infinitive** (to want to …) – e.g. **quiero estudiar** en un nuevo instituto (I want to study in a new school)
* **tener ganas de + infinitive** (to want to …) – e.g. **tengo ganas de ir** a la universidad (I want to go to university)
* **esperar + infinitive** (to hope to …) – e.g. **espero sacar** buenas notas (I hope to get good grades)
* **tener la intención de + infinitive** (to intend to …) – e.g. **tengo la intención de continuar** con mis estudios (I intend to continue with my studies)

You can also use **quisiera/me gustaría** to say what you would like to do.

EXAM TASK

Answer the questions in English.

Conviértete en un profesional cualificado en liderazgo y visión global. Consigue un título superior y prepárate para acceder a una profesión en dos años. Te ofrecemos apoyo personalizado, un mentor personal y conexión con más de 2.700 empresas.

La calidad de los profesores, el uso de tecnología en las clases, el enfoque internacional en un campus, la mejora de tu nivel de inglés y la posibilidad de realizar intercambios internacionales, todos te ayudarán a convertirte en un gran profesional.

1. What will you learn about on the course? Give **one** detail.
2. How long does the course last?
3. What do they offer? Give **two** details.
4. What will help turn you into a professional? Give **three** details.

CAREER PLANS

En el futuro espero hacer muchas cosas y vivir muchas experiencias.

In the future I hope to do many things and have many experiences.

Cuando termine mis estudios, buscaré un trabajo con un salario alto.

When I finish my studies, I will look for a job with a high salary.

Preferiría trabajar para mí mismo y ser mi propio jefe.

I would prefer to work for myself and be my own boss.

Voy a ahorrar mucho dinero para comprar una casa.

I am going to save lots of money to buy a house.

Siempre he querido ser profesor/a porque el trabajo me inspira.

I've always wanted to be a teacher as the work inspires me.

Espero encontrar un trabajo cerca/lejos de donde vivo.

I hope to find a job near to/far from where I live.

Tengo que admitir que no tengo ninguna idea de lo que quiero hacer en el futuro.

I must admit that I don't have any idea what I would like to do in the future.

Todavía no he decidido lo que voy a hacer como trabajo.

I haven't yet decided what job I want to do.

Como todo el mundo, no quiero estar en paro.

Like everyone, I don't want to be unemployed.

No quiero un trabajo monótono.

I don't want to have a monotonous job.

Estoy abierto/a a nuevas oportunidades.

I am open to new opportunities.

No tengo ni la más remota idea de qué hacer con mi vida.

I don't have the remotest idea what to do with my life.

Quisiera encontrar un trabajo que me apasione.

I would like to find a job that I am passionate about.

Después de mis estudios, me gustaría vivir en Australia.

After my studies, I would like to live in Australia.

Espero trabajar en el extranjero para mejorar mis conocimientos lingüísticos.

I hope to work abroad to improve my language skills.

Cuando tenía diez años mi sueño era ser astronauta.

When I was ten, I dreamt of becoming an astronaut.

Hace unos años tenía la intención de estudiar contabilidad.

A few years ago, I intended to study accountancy.

Siempre me han interesado los negocios.

I have always been interested in business.

Si tuviera la oportunidad, estudiaría un máster al acabar la carrera.

If I had the chance, I would study for a master's after my degree.

Cuando era más joven quería ser profesor/a, pero ahora preferiría estudiar medicina.

When I was younger I wanted to be a teacher, but now I would prefer to study medicine.

Some useful time phrases for talking about your future plans include:

en el futuro – in the future

en primer lugar – in the first place

luego – then

después de terminar mis estudios – after finishing my studies

al acabar la carrera – on finishing my degree

en los próximos cinco años – in the next five years

a corto plazo – in the short term

a largo plazo – in the long term

más adelante – further ahead

Translate the following paragraph into Spanish:

EXAM TASK

I want to travel to lots of places after university. In the short term, I would like to spend a gap year abroad. I hope to work in an international organisation and learn about different cultures. It would be an unforgettable experience. When I was younger, I always wanted to learn a new language.

GRAMMAR

GRAMMAR TERMS

It's important to understand what these terms mean as they will be used regularly throughout your GCSE course.

Adjectives: Adjectives describe nouns. They answer the questions: which, what kind of, how many – e.g. big.

Adverbs: Adverbs describe verbs (and sometimes adjectives and other adverbs). They answer the questions: how, when, where – e.g. regularly.

Articles: These include the definite article (the) and the indefinite article (a/an).

Comparative: This is a form of an adjective used when comparing two things – e.g. better.

Connective/Conjunction: This is a word or phrase that connects two ideas or parts of a sentence – e.g. because.

Demonstratives: These are words that demonstrate (point out) – e.g. this, that, these, those.

Gender: Used for nouns to say if they're masculine or feminine.

Imperative: A form of a verb used when giving instructions or commands – e.g. stop!

Infinitive: This is the form of verb you find in the dictionary. In English it always has the word 'to' in front of it – e.g. to study – and in Spanish it ends in ar, er or ir.

Irregular verb: A verb that does not follow regular patterns and has a different form when conjugated. These usually need to be learned by heart.

Noun: A person, place, thing or idea.

Object: The object is the person/thing in a sentence which has the action happen to it.

Plural: More than one of an item.

Possessive: These are words that imply ownership – e.g. my house.

Prepositions: These are words that help describe something's location or give other information – e.g. in, on.

Pronouns: These are words which take the place of nouns in a sentence.

Reflexive verbs: Reflexive verbs describe actions the subject of the sentence does to themselves – e.g. vestirse (to get dressed).

Singular: Refers to only one of an item (as opposed to plural for more than one).

Subject: The person/thing in the sentence which is doing the action.

Superlative: The superlative is *the most* of something – e.g. best, worst, biggest.

Synonyms: Words which share the same meaning are synonyms.

Tense: This is a change in the verb to describe actions happening in the past, present, future or conditional.

Verbs: These are the action words which are doing something in a sentence.

Don't panic when you see the following grammar list! This is a list of **every** grammar point that might come up at GCSE. You won't need to use all of these grammar points yourself, but it will help if you are able to recognise different linguistic features. This reference section means that you can look up any grammar terms that are confusing you. There are also some grammar exercises throughout so that you can practise your knowledge. The verb tables at the back of this section will be useful when you are revising for your speaking and writing exams.

NOUNS

MASCULINE AND FEMININE

Nouns are words that name things, people, places and ideas. In Spanish, all nouns are either masculine or feminine.

Usually, nouns that end in o are masculine and nouns that end in a are feminine, but there are some exceptions – e.g. el problema, el planeta, la mano, la foto.

Nouns ending in or, ón and és tend to be masculine whereas nouns ending in ión, dad and tad are usually feminine.

SINGULAR AND PLURAL

To make nouns plural, you usually:

- Add s to nouns ending in a vowel – e.g. libro → libros
- Add es to nouns ending in a consonant – e.g. ciudad → ciudades
- Remove the z and add ces to nouns ending in a z – e.g. vez → veces
- Add es to nouns ending in ión but get rid of the accent – e.g. región → regiones

ARTICLES

DEFINITE ARTICLES (EL/LA/LOS/LAS)

In Spanish, the word for 'the' changes depending on whether the noun it goes with is masculine, feminine, singular or plural – e.g. **el** hermano → **los** hermanos, **la** casa → **las** casas.

INDEFINITE ARTICLES (UN/UNA/UNOS/UNAS)

The word for 'a/an' or 'some' also depends on whether the noun it goes with is masculine, feminine, singular or plural – e.g. **un** coche → **unos** coches, **una** revista → **unas** revistas.

You don't need to use the indefinite article when you are talking about jobs – e.g. mi primo es profesor – or when it comes after the verb tener in negative sentences – e.g. no tengo abrigo.

THE NEUTER ARTICLE (LO)

You can use lo + **adjective** to mean 'the … thing'. The adjective after lo is always masculine and singular – e.g. lo importante (the important thing).

You can also use lo + **adjective** + es que as a really good way to start a sentence – e.g. lo positivo es que … (the positive thing is that …) or you can use lo + **adjective** + es + **infinitive** – e.g. lo bueno es ganar dinero (the good thing is earning money).

ADJECTIVES

MAKING ADJECTIVES AGREE WITH THE NOUN

In Spanish, all adjectives (words that describe nouns, people, places and things) have different endings depending on whether the word they are describing is masculine, feminine, singular or plural. In other words, adjectives always have to agree with the noun. They usually follow these patterns:

Adjectives ending in:	Masculine singular	Feminine singular	Masculine plural	Feminine plural
o/a	pequeño	pequeña	pequeños	pequeñas
e	grande	grande	grandes	grandes
or/ora	trabajador	trabajadora	trabajadores	trabajadoras
a consonant	azul	azul	azules	azules

Adjectives of nationality often end in o and follow the same patterns as in the table. Some adjectives of nationality that end in a consonant follow a slightly different pattern:

Ending in s	inglés	inglesa	ingleses	inglesas
Ending in l	español	española	españoles	españolas

Some adjectives don't change at all – e.g. rosa, naranja, cada.

POSITION OF ADJECTIVES

Most adjectives in Spanish go after the noun they are describing – e.g. un instituto grande, but some always come before – e.g. poco, mucho, próximo, ultimo, alguno, ninguno, primero, segundo, tercera.

Some adjectives are shortened when they come in front of a masculine singular noun:

> bueno → buen – good – e.g. es un **buen** colegio
> malo → mal – bad – e.g. hace **mal** tiempo
> primero → primer – first – e.g. es el **primer** día
> tercero → tercer – third – e.g. es mi **tercer** examen del día
> alguno → algún – some/any – e.g. prefiero hacer **algún** deporte
> ninguno → ningún – none – e.g. no tengo **ningún** libro

Notice that an accent is added on algún and ningún.

The meaning of grande (big) changes to mean 'great' when it comes before a noun. It is also shortened before masculine and feminine nouns – e.g. un **gran** colegio, una **gran** película.

COMPARATIVES AND SUPERLATIVES

You use comparative adjectives to compare two things and say one is bigger, smaller, better, etc. than the other. Superlative adjectives are used to compare two things and say which one is the best, worst, biggest, etc. To form the comparative you can use the following structures:

- más + **adjective** + que (more … than) – e.g. Madrid es **más grande que** Toledo (Madrid is bigger than Toledo)
- menos + **adjective** + que (less … than) – e.g. el campo es **menos ruidoso que** la ciudad (the countryside is less noisy than the city)
- tan + **adjective** + como (as … as) – e.g. la película es **tan interesante como** el libro (the film is as interesting as the book)

The superlative is formed by using the correct form of the adjective with the following structure:

- el/la/los/las + más/menos + **adjective** – e.g. mi casa es **la más grande** (my house is the biggest)

There are also irregular comparatives and superlatives – e.g. es la **peor** asignatura (it's the worst subject):

Adjective	Comparative	Superlative
bueno (good)	mejor (better)	el/la mejor, los/las mejores (the best)
malo (bad)	peor (worse)	el/la peor, los/las peores (the worst)

There are also two other special sorts of irregular comparatives – mayor is used for 'older' and menor for 'younger', usually when referring to brothers and sisters – e.g. mi hermano **mayor** (my older brother), mis hermanas **menores** (my younger sisters).

To add extra emphasis to an adjective you can also add the ending ísimo after removing the final vowel (where necessary) – e.g. bueno → buenísimo, malo → malísimo. These are called absolute superlatives.

GRAMMAR

Translate the following sentences into English.
1. Para mí, lo más importante es ayudar a los demás.
2. Creo que el peor problema es la inmigración.
3. En mi opinión, la pobreza es más grave que el conflicto.
4. La inmigración es tan seria como el terrorismo.
5. Considero que la situación más urgente es la crisis económica.
6. Es más fácil vender pasteles que pedir donaciones.

DEMONSTRATIVE ADJECTIVES (THIS, THAT, THESE, THOSE)

There are three groups of demonstrative adjectives in Spanish. They need to agree with the noun they are describing – e.g. me gustan **estos** pasteles (I like these cakes).

	this/these	that/those (near)	that/those (further away)
Masculine singular	este	ese	aquel
Feminine singular	esta	esa	aquella
Masculine plural	estos	esos	aquellos
Feminine plural	estas	esas	aquellas

INDEFINITE ADJECTIVES

The most common indefinite adjectives you will use are **cada** (each/every), **otro** (another/other), **todo** (each/every/all), **mismo** (same) and **alguno** (some/a few/any). They all need to agree with the noun they are describing except **cada**, which never changes.

RELATIVE ADJECTIVES (CUYO, CUYA, CUYOS, CUYAS)

Cuyo means 'whose' and has to agree with the noun that follows it – e.g. el colegio, **cuyos** profesores son muy buenos … (the school, whose teachers are very good …).

POSSESSIVE ADJECTIVES

We use possessive adjectives to express ownership – e.g. my, your, his. Possessive adjectives must agree with the noun that follows them – **not** the person who 'owns' the noun – e.g. **mis** padres (my parents), **tus** amigos (your friends), **nuestro** profesor (our teacher).

	Singular	Plural
my	mi	mis
your (singular)	tu	tus
his/her/its	su	sus
our	nuestro/a	nuestros/as
your (plural)	vuestro/a	vuestros/as
their	su	sus

INTERROGATIVE ADJECTIVES

Use ¿Qué? to ask 'What?' – e.g. ¿**Qué** te gusta hacer? (What do you like doing?) It never changes.

Use ¿Cuál? to ask 'Which?' It needs to agree with the noun that follows it – e.g. ¿**Cuáles** asignaturas prefieres? (Which subjects do you like?)

Use ¿Cuánto? to ask 'How much?' It also needs to agree with the noun that follows it – e.g. ¿**Cuántas** asignaturas estudias? (How many subjects do you study?)

ADVERBS

FORMING ADVERBS

Adverbs are usually used to describe a verb to express how, when, where or to what extent something is happening. In other words, they describe how an action is done (quickly, regularly, badly, etc.) – e.g. **juego al tenis raramente** (I rarely play tennis).

Many Spanish adverbs are formed by adding **mente** to the feminine form of the adjective – e.g. **fácil → fácilmente**.

Some adverbs are completely irregular – e.g. **bien** (well), **mal** (badly) – e.g. **habla español muy bien** (he speaks Spanish very well).

GRAMMAR

Make these adjectives into adverbs and write a sentence in Spanish using each one.
1. tranquilo
2. rápido
3. activo
4. frecuente
5. malsano

COMPARATIVE AND SUPERLATIVE ADVERBS

As with adjectives, you can make comparisons with adverbs using **más que** and **menos que** – e.g. **llego menos rápidamente en tren que en autobús** (I arrive less quickly by train than by bus).

Similarly, you can also use superlative adverbs – e.g. **ir al cine es la actividad que hago más regularmente** (going to the cinema is the activity I do most often).

ADVERBS OF TIME AND PLACE

Some useful irregular adverbs include:

hoy – today
mañana – tomorrow
ayer – yesterday
ahora – now
ya – already
a veces – sometimes
a menudo – often
siempre – always
aquí – here
allí – there

QUANTIFIERS AND INTENSIFIERS

Try to add detail to your Spanish by including quantifiers and intensifiers – e.g.:

> bastante – enough
> demasiado – too (much)
> un poco – a little
> mucho – a lot
> muy – very

> e.g. Mi colegio es **un poco** antiguo. Los profesores son **demasiado** estrictos.

You have to be careful with demasiado as it can be an adjective as well as an adverb, which means that sometimes it has to agree with the noun it is describing – e.g. los deberes son **demasiado** dificiles (homework is too hard). Demasiado is describing difícil, which means it's an adverb and doesn't change.

But if you said tenemos **demasiados** deberes (we have too much homework), demasiado is describing los deberes, which means it's an adjective and it has to agree.

INTERROGATIVE ADVERBS

These question words all have an accent:

> ¿Cómo? – How?
> ¿Cuándo? – When?
> ¿Dónde? – Where?

PRONOUNS

SUBJECT PRONOUNS

The words I, you, he, she, we and they are subject pronouns. They are only really used for emphasis in Spanish:

yo – I
nosotros/as – we
tú – you (singular)
vosotros/as – you (plural)
él – he
ella – she
ellos/as – they
usted – you (formal singular)
ustedes – you (formal plural)

Remember that there are different ways of saying 'you' in Spanish. Use tú when you are talking to one person and vosotros when you are talking to more than one person. You use usted and ustedes to mean 'you' in formal situations (e.g. in a job interview, talking to your head teacher, talking to someone you don't know).

OBJECT PRONOUNS

There are two types of object pronouns: direct and indirect.

Direct object pronouns are used to replace a noun that is not the subject of the verb – e.g. using 'it' instead of the noun itself. They are:

me – me
te – you
lo – him/it
la – her/it
nos – us
os – you
los/las – them

Indirect object pronouns are used to replace a noun which is not the direct object of the verb – e.g. Les escribe (I wrote to them). They are:

me – (to) me
te – (to) you
le – (to) him/her/it
nos – (to) us
os – (to) you
les – (to) them

Direct and indirect object pronouns come in front of the verb – e.g. **lo** hice (I did it), **los** compré (I bought them), **le** voy a escribir (I am going to write to him), los profesores **nos** dan mucho trabajo (the teachers give us a lot of work). They also come after a negative word – e.g. no **lo** tengo (I don't have it).

They also go at the end of an infinitive/gerund or at the beginning of the sentence when used in the immediate future or present continuous tense – e.g. voy a comprar**lo/lo** voy a comprar (I am going to buy it) or estoy haciéndo**lo/lo** estoy haciendo (I am doing it).

If you use two pronouns in the same sentence, the indirect object pronoun always comes before the direct object pronoun – e.g. mis amigos **me** lo dieron (my friends gave it to **me**).

REFLEXIVE PRONOUNS

You use reflexive pronouns (me, te, se, nos, os, se) when the subject and the object of the verb are the same. They come before the verb – e.g. **me** visto (I get myself dressed), **nos** levantamos (we get ourselves up).

RELATIVE PRONOUNS (QUE, QUIEN, LO QUE, EL QUE, EL CUAL)

You use relative pronouns to link phrases together.

- Que can refer to people or things and means 'who', 'that' or 'which'. We often leave this out in English but you always have to include it in Spanish – e.g. el chico **que** vive en la misma calle (the boy who lives in the same street), las asignaturas **que** estudio (the subjects that I study).
- Quien and quienes (plural) mean 'who' and can only be used for people – e.g. mi hermano, **quien** es estudiante, no vive en casa (my brother, who is a student, doesn't live at home), mis profesores, **quienes** son muy estrictos, nos dan muchos deberes (my teachers, who are very strict, give us lots of homework). This is very rarely used in spoken language, and que is often used instead.
- Lo que is used to mean 'what' (or 'that which') when you are talking about a general idea – e.g. **lo que** no me gusta de mi colegio es que los profesores son estrictos (what I don't like about my school is that the teachers are strict), **lo que** prefiero es escuchar música (what I prefer is listening to music).
- You use el que, la que, los que and las que to refer to both people and things – e.g. mi profesor, **el que** enseña historia, es muy gracioso (my teacher, the one who teaches history, is very funny), mis vecinos, **los que** viven en la casa enorme, tienen mucho dinero (my neighbours, the ones who live in the enormous house, have lots of money).
- El cual, la cual, los cuales and las cuales mean exactly the same thing as el que, la que, los que and las que and work in exactly the same way. They aren't really used much in conversation but you might see them in written texts.

DISJUNCTIVE PRONOUNS

Disjunctive pronouns (mí, ti, él, ella, usted, nosotros/as, vosotros/as, ellos/as, ustedes) are also called emphatic pronouns because you use them for emphasis – e.g. para **mí**, lo más importante es ... (for me, the most important thing is …), para **nosotros**, las vacaciones son esenciales (for us, holidays are essential), a **mí**, no me gusta el uniforme (me, I don't like the uniform).

There is a special form you use for 'with me' and 'with you'. You use conmigo for 'with me' – e.g. mis amigos vienen **conmigo** (my friends are coming with me) and contigo for 'with you' (tú) – e.g. ¿Puedo venir **contigo**? (Can I come with you?)

POSSESSIVE PRONOUNS

Instead of using a possessive and a noun to say 'my book', 'your house', 'his car', etc. you can use a possessive pronoun to say 'mine', 'yours', 'his', etc. They need to agree with the noun they are replacing, depending on whether it is masculine, feminine, singular or plural.

	Masculine singular	Feminine singular	Masculine plural	Feminine plural
mine	el mío	la mía	los míos	las mías
yours	el tuyo	la tuya	los tuyos	las tuyas
his/hers/its	el suyo	la suya	los suyos	las suyas
ours	el nuestro	la nuestra	los nuestros	las nuestras
yours (plural)	el vuestro	la vuestra	los vuestros	las vuestras
theirs	el suyo	la suya	los suyos	las suyas

DEMONSTRATIVE PRONOUNS

Demonstrative pronouns are used instead of a noun to avoid repeating it. You use the same words as demonstrative adjectives. You will sometimes see them written with accents, following old spelling conventions, but these are the forms you need to learn to use.

	this one/these ones	that one/those ones (near)	that one/those ones (further away)
Masculine singular	este	ese	aquel
Feminine singular	esta	esa	aquella
Masculine plural	estos	esos	aquellos
Feminine plural	estas	esas	aquellas

You can also use esto, eso and aquello to refer to a general idea – e.g. **eso** no me interesa (that doesn't interest me), **esto** me parece importante (this seems important to me).

It's also useful to know aquí (here), allí (there) and allá (over there, meaning further away).

INDEFINITE PRONOUNS

The Spanish for 'something' is algo – e.g. me gustaría hacer **algo** relacionado con la tecnología (I would like to do something related to technology).

The Spanish for 'someone' is alguien – e.g. busco a **alguien** importante (I am looking for someone important).

INTERROGATIVE PRONOUNS

Interrogative pronouns – such as cuál(es) (what/which one(s)), qué (what) and quién(es) (who) – usually come at the start of a sentence – e.g. **¿Cuál es tu asignatura preferida?** (What is your favourite subject?), **¿Quiénes son tus mejores amigos?** (Who are your best friends?)

If you use a preposition with these question words, then the preposition comes first:

¿De qué? – About/of what?
¿A quién(es)? – Whom?
¿Con quién(es)? – With whom?
¿De quién(es)? – Whose?
¿Por qué? – Why? (Meaning: for what reason?)
¿Para qué? – Why? (Meaning: for what purpose?)

PREPOSITIONS

COMMON PREPOSITIONS

Prepositions are linking words which usually show direction, location or time. The most common prepositions are:

a – to/at
con – with
de – of/from
en – in/on/at

Some common prepositions of time include:

antes de – before
después de – after
hasta – until

Because the following prepositions relate to location or direction, you usually see them after the verb estar:

cerca de – near
al lado de – next to
delante de – in front of
dentro de – inside
detrás de – behind
encima de – on top of
enfrente de – opposite
entre – between
fuera de – outside of
lejos de – far from

POR AND PARA

Por and para both mean 'for' but they are used in different ways. Por usually refers to movement through time or places, whereas para refers to destinations or purposes.

Por has many uses but you will see it used most often to mean 'through', 'along' and 'per'. It can be used in the following ways:

- To describe motion or place – e.g. caminan **por** las calles (they walk through the streets).
- To describe how something is done – e.g. lo envío **por** correo electrónico (I'm sending it by e-mail).
- To mean 'per' – e.g. me pagan cinco libras **por** hora (they pay me five pounds per hour).

Here are some common phrases that you will see with por:

por ejemplo – for example
por favor – please
por ciento – per cent
por supuesto – of course
por lo tanto – therefore

The preposition para is used, amongst other things, to mean 'in order to', 'for the purpose of' and 'intended for'. It can show the following things:

- The destination/person something is intended for – e.g. el café es **para** mi madre (the coffee is for my mother).
- Purposes/goals – e.g. trabajo muy duro **para** sacar buenas notas (I work very hard in order to get good grades).
- Opinions – e.g. **para** mí, es muy importante (for me, it's very important).

COMMON CONJUNCTIONS

Conjunctions or connectives are used to form extended sentences and can be used to add more detail to your written and spoken Spanish. The most common are:

y – and
pero – but
o – or
porque – because
si – if
también – also

Remember that y changes to e before words beginning with i or hi – e.g. estudio francés **e** inglés (I study French and English).

O changes to u before words beginning with o or ho – e.g. trabajo siete **u** ocho horas (I work seven or eight hours).

Some other useful connectives include:

además – furthermore/what's more
así que – so/therefore
aunque – although
mientras – while/meanwhile
por lo tanto – therefore
sin embargo – however

PERSONAL A

When the object of a verb is a person – e.g. I am looking for Alex, I saw Luisa in the shop – you need to include the personal **a** before naming that person – e.g. busco **a** Alex, vi **a** Luisa en la tienda.

TIME EXPRESSIONS

DESDE HACE

You can use desde hace with the present tense to say how long you have been doing something – e.g. **Juego al tenis desde hace** cinco años (I've been playing tennis for five years). You can also use **desde** on its own to mean 'since' or 'from'.

GRAMMAR

Translate the following sentences into English:
1. Juego al tenis desde hace seis meses.
2. Soy vegetariano desde hace tres años.
3. Jorge juega al baloncesto desde pequeño.
4. Vivo aquí desde mi nacimiento.

DESDE HACÍA

If you want to say how long you had been doing something in the past, you can use **desde hacía** with the imperfect tense – e.g. jugaba al baloncesto **desde hacía** tres meses (I had been playing basketball for three months).

VERBS AND TENSES

PRESENT TENSE

The present tense is used to talk about what usually happens – e.g. normalmente **juego** al fútbol (I normally play football), what things are like – e.g. mi colegio **tiene** mil alumnos (my school has a thousand pupils), and what is happening now – e.g. **hago** mis deberes (I'm doing my homework).

REGULAR VERBS

To form the present tense of regular ar, er and ir verbs, you cross off the **ar/er/ir** and add the following endings:

	escuchar – to listen	**beber** – to drink	**vivir** – to live
yo	escuch**o**	beb**o**	viv**o**
tú	escuch**as**	beb**es**	viv**es**
él/ella/usted	escuch**a**	beb**e**	viv**e**
nosotros	escuch**amos**	beb**emos**	viv**imos**
vosotros	escuch**áis**	beb**éis**	viv**ís**
ellos/ellas/ustedes	escuch**an**	beb**en**	viv**en**

See pages 142–143 for a list of common regular ar, er and ir verbs that all follow these patterns.

GRAMMAR

Complete these sentences with the correct present tense form of the regular verbs in brackets.

1. Mi hermano _____ (vivir) con su novia.
2. Mis amigos _____ (hablar) demasiado.
3. Cada noche yo _____ (chatear) en Internet.
4. Mi familia y yo siempre _____ (cenar) juntos.
5. Yo _____ (creer) que la amistad es importante.
6. Los jóvenes _____ (utilizar) la tecnología todo el tiempo.

RADICAL-CHANGING VERBS

These verbs are conjugated in the same way as regular verbs (cross off the **ar/er/ir** and add the present tense endings) but the stem changes in every form of the verb apart from **nosotros** and **vosotros**. There are three main groups of radical-changing verbs:

	u/o → ue	e → ie	e → i
	e.g. **dormir** – to sleep	e.g. **empezar** – to start	e.g. **repetir** – to repeat
yo	d**ue**rmo	emp**ie**zo	rep**i**to
tú	d**ue**rmes	emp**ie**zas	rep**i**tes
él/ella/usted	d**ue**rme	emp**ie**za	rep**i**te
nosotros	dormimos	empezamos	repetimos
vosotros	dormís	empezáis	repetís
ellos/ellas/ustedes	d**ue**rmen	emp**ie**zan	rep**i**ten

Other examples of verbs that follow these patterns are:

u/o → ue	
Infinitive	yo form
jugar – to play	j**ue**go
poder – to be able	p**ue**do
acostarse – to go to bed	me ac**ue**sto
encontrar – to find/meet	enc**ue**ntro
volver – to return	v**ue**lvo

e → ie	
Infinitive	yo form
despertarse – to wake up	me desp**ie**rto
entender – to understand	ent**ie**ndo
pensar – to think	p**ie**nso
perder – to lose	p**ie**rdo
preferir – to prefer	pref**ie**ro
querer – to want	qu**ie**ro
recomendar – to recommend	recom**ie**ndo

e → i	
Infinitive	**yo form**
pedir – to ask for	**pi**do
servir – to serve	**sir**vo
vestirse – to get dressed	me **vi**sto

IRREGULAR VERBS

Irregular verbs don't follow the normal patterns of regular **ar**, **er** and **ir** verbs. You need to learn these by heart. The two most common irregular verbs are:

	ser – to be	**ir – to go**
yo	soy	voy
tú	eres	vas
él/ella/usted	es	va
nosotros	somos	vamos
vosotros	sois	vais
ellos/ellas/ustedes	son	van

Look at the verb tables on pages 144–146 for other irregular verbs – e.g. **decir** (to say), **venir** (to come) and **ver** (to see). Some verbs are irregular in the **yo** form but follow the regular present tense patterns in the other forms:

Infinitive	**yo form**
conducir – to drive	conduzco
conocer – to know	conozco
dar – to give	doy
estar – to be	estoy
hacer – to make/do	hago
poner – to put	pongo
saber – to know	sé
salir – to go out	salgo
tener – to have	tengo
traer – to bring	traigo

GRAMMAR

Complete these sentences with the correct present tense form of the irregular or radical-changing verb in brackets.

1. Mi hermana _____ (preferir) salir con sus amigos.
2. Irma no _____ (tener) muchos deberes.
3. Mis tíos _____ (querer) separarse.
4. Nosotros _____ (poder) salir hasta muy tarde.
5. Mis padres _____ (ser) muy estrictos.

REFLEXIVE VERBS

Reflexive verbs describe an action that you do to yourself. They work in the same way as other verbs but need to be preceded by a reflexive pronoun (me, te, se, nos, os, se).

	levantarse – to get up
yo	**me** levanto
tú	**te** levantas
él/ella/usted	**se** levanta
nosotros	**nos** levantamos
vosotros	**os** levantáis
ellos/ellas/ustedes	**se** levantan

In the infinitive, the reflexive pronoun goes at the end of the verb – e.g. ducharse. If you are using an infinitive in a construction – e.g. tener que + **infinitive** – then you will need to change the reflexive pronoun to match the person doing the action – e.g. tengo que levantarme temprano (I have to get up early tomorrow).

PHRASES USING SE

You can use se in certain phrases:

- se puede + **infinitive** (you can …) – e.g. **se** puede visitar el museo (you can visit the museum)
- se debe + **infinitive** (you must …) – e.g. **se** deben hacer los deberes (you must do homework)
- se necesita + **infinitive or noun** (you need …) – e.g. **se** necesita trabajar muy duro (you need to work very hard), **se** necesita mucho dinero (you need a lot of money)
- se habla de + **noun** (you/people talk about …) – e.g. **se** habla del problema de la pobreza (people talk about the problem of poverty)

IMPERSONAL VERBS

Gustar (to like) and encantar (to love) are impersonal verbs and don't work in the same way as other verbs.

Use gusta/encanta for single things or an activity (using a verb) – e.g. me **gusta** la ropa (I like clothes), me **encanta** diseñar (I love designing).

Use gustan/encantan for two or more things – e.g. me **gustan** los deportes (I like sports), me **encantan** la ropa y la joyería (I love clothes and jewellery).

You also need to use indirect object pronouns (me, te, le, nos, os, les) in front of the verb to say who is doing the liking – e.g. **le** gusta (he likes it), **nos** gustan (we like them).

Use mucho to say you like something a lot – e.g. me gusta **mucho**.

USES OF **SER** AND **ESTAR**

Both ser and estar mean 'to be' but in different ways.

Ser is used with physical description, personality and character, nationality, race, gender, professions, what things are made of, dates, days, seasons, time and possession – e.g. **soy** alto (I am tall), **es** el ocho de diciembre (it's the eighth of December).

Estar is used with feelings, moods, emotions, physical conditions or appearances, marital status and location of things and people – e.g. **estoy** cansada (I am tired), **están** separados (they are separated).

GRAMMAR

Choose the correct verb – can you explain your choice?
1. Cada persona **es/está** diferente.
2. Algunos padres **son/están** preocupados por sus hijos.
3. Mi hermana **es/está** alta y guapa.
4. Prefiero **ser/estar** con mis amigos.
5. Both of these pairs of phrases are correct – can you work out what they mean?
   a. Es aburrido. Estoy aburrida.
   b. Marina es bonita. Marina está bonita.

NEGATIVES

To make a sentence negative you usually put no before the verb – e.g. **no** tengo hermanos (I don't have any brothers or sisters).

Another common negative word is nunca, which means 'never'. It can go at the start of the sentence instead of no – e.g. **nunca** voy a tener hijos (I'm never going to have children) – or you can put no at the start and nunca at the end of the sentence – e.g. **no** voy a tener hijos **nunca**.

Other negatives include:

nada – nothing
e.g. no tengo **nada** – I don't have anything

nadie – nobody
e.g. **nadie** fue a la fiesta – nobody went to the party

ningún (-o, -a, -os, -as) – no/none
e.g. no tengo **ningunos** deberes – I don't have any homework

tampoco – neither
e.g. no me gusta la historia **tampoco** – I don't like history either

ni ... ni – neither ... nor
e.g. no me gusta **ni** el tenis **ni** el rugby – I don't like tennis or rugby

GERUNDS

The gerund is also called the present participle. It is the equivalent of the ing form in English – e.g. swimming, dancing, playing.

To form the gerund of ar verbs you take off the ar and add ando – e.g. hablar → habl**ando**.

To form the gerund of er/ir verbs you take off the er/ir and add iendo – e.g. beber → beb**iendo**, vivir → viv**iendo**.

Look at the verb tables on pages 144–146 for irregular gerunds. Here are some examples:

dormir (to sleep) → durmiendo (sleeping)
leer (to read) → leyendo (reading)
ir (to go) → yendo (going)
ser (to be) → siendo (being)

Be careful because sometimes we use a gerund in English when you would use an infinitive in Spanish – e.g. me gusta **nadar** (I like swimming).

PRESENT CONTINUOUS TENSE

The present continuous is used to say what is happening at the time of speaking. The gerund is used with the present tense of the verb **estar** to form the present continuous – e.g. **estoy haciendo** mis deberes (I am doing my homework).

	Present tense of **estar**	Gerund
yo	estoy	hablando, estudiando, escuchando, música, etc.
tú	estás	
él/ella/usted	está	
nosotros	estamos	
vosotros	estáis	
ellos/ellas/ustedes	están	

IMMEDIATE FUTURE TENSE

Ir a + **infinitive** is a really useful way to include another tense in your Spanish. It's called the immediate future and it's used to say what you are going to do or what is going to happen – e.g. **voy a tener** hijos dentro de diez años (I'm going to have children in ten years). It is formed with the present tense of ir followed by the infinitive.

	Present tense of **ir**	a	Infinitive
yo	voy		salir, visitar, vivir, etc.
tú	vas		
él/ella/usted	va		
nosotros	vamos		
vosotros	vais		
ellos/ellas/ustedes	van		

GRAMMAR

Translate these sentences into Spanish:
1. I am going to have children.
2. We are going to live in a big house.
3. My friends are going to write a blog.
4. My sister is going to go out with her boyfriend.

FUTURE TENSE

The future tense is used to say what will happen. To form the future tense, add the correct ending to the infinitive of the verb.

	ar verbs – e.g.: estudi**ar** – to study	**er** verbs – e.g.: aprend**er** – to learn	**ir** verbs – e.g.: viv**ir** – to live
yo	estudiar**é**	aprender**é**	vivir**é**
tú	estudiar**ás**	aprender**ás**	vivir**ás**
él/ella/usted	estudiar**á**	aprender**á**	vivir**á**
nosotros	estudiar**emos**	aprender**emos**	vivir**emos**
vosotros	estudiar**éis**	aprender**éis**	vivir**éis**
ellos/ellas/ustedes	estudiar**án**	aprender**án**	vivir**án**

All verbs use the same endings but for some verbs you add the endings on to an irregular form of the stem – e.g. hacer → **har**é, salir → **sald**ré, tener → **tend**ré. Check the irregular verb tables on pages 144–146 for more irregular verbs in the future tense.

Translate these sentences into English:
1. Viviré en un piso con mis amigos.
2. Mañana compraré un móvil nuevo.
3. La tecnología será más importante en el futuro.
4. Mis padres no estarán muy contentos.

CONDITIONAL TENSE

You use the conditional in Spanish to say 'would'. The conditional verb that you will likely use most often is me gustaría (I would like).

The conditional tense is formed by adding the conditional endings to the infinitive of the verb.

	ar verbs – e.g.: estudi**ar** – to study	**er** verbs – e.g.: aprend**er** – to learn	**ir** verbs – e.g.: **vivir** – to live
yo	estudiar**ía**	aprender**ía**	vivir**ía**
tú	estudiar**ías**	aprender**ías**	vivir**ías**
él/ella/usted	estudiar**ía**	aprender**ía**	vivir**ía**
nosotros	estudiar**íamos**	aprender**íamos**	vivir**íamos**
vosotros	estudiar**íais**	aprender**íais**	vivir**íais**
ellos/ellas/ustedes	estudiar**ían**	aprender**ían**	vivir**ían**

Verbs which are irregular in the conditional are also irregular in the future tense. See the verb tables on pages 144–146.

Choose the correct conditional verb from the list to complete each sentence.
1. En el futuro _____ estudiar el español.
2. _____ buenas notas en mis exámenes.
3. Mi profesor ideal _____ divertido.
4. Mi colegio ideal _____ instalaciones modernas.
5. _____ en la universidad.
6. Mis amigos _____ al club de baloncesto.

sería	sacaría	me gustaría
irían	tendría	estudiaría

PRETERITE

You use the preterite to talk about completed actions in the past – e.g. **fui al cine** (I went to the cinema), **hice mis deberes** (I did my homework).

The preterite is formed by crossing the ai/ir/er endings off the infinitive and adding the preterite endings.

	ar verbs – e.g.: hab**lar** – **to speak**	**er** verbs – e.g.: co**mer** – **to eat**	**ir** verbs – e.g.: reci**bir** – **to receive**
yo	habl**é**	com**í**	recib**í**
tú	habl**aste**	com**iste**	recib**iste**
él/ella/usted	habl**ó**	com**ió**	recib**ió**
nosotros	habl**amos**	com**imos**	recib**imos**
vosotros	habl**asteis**	com**isteis**	recib**isteis**
ellos/ellas/ustedes	habl**aron**	com**ieron**	recib**ieron**

GRAMMAR

Complete the sentences using the preterite form of the verb in brackets.
1. La semana pasada nosotros _____ (visitar) los monumentos.
2. Ayer _____ (yo, viajar) al colegio en coche.
3. Mis padres _____ (comprar) un billete.
4. Ayer _____ (yo, salir) con mis amigos.
5. ¿Cómo _____ (tú, viajar) de vacaciones el año pasado?

The most common irregular verbs in the preterite are:

	ser/ir – to be/to go	**hacer** – to make/do	**tener** – to have
yo	fui	hice	tuve
tú	fuiste	hiciste	tuviste
él/ella/usted	fue	hizo	tuvo
nosotros	fuimos	hicimos	tuvimos
vosotros	fuisteis	hicisteis	tuvisteis
ellos/ellas/ustedes	fueron	hicieron	tuvieron

See the verb tables on pages 144–146 for more irregular verbs in the preterite – e.g. **estar** (to be), **ver** (to see) and **dar** (to give).

Some verbs in the preterite have irregular spellings in the yo form – e.g.:

> empezar (to start/begin) → empecé
> jugar (to play) → jugué
> llegar (to arrive) → llegué

Some verbs in the preterite have irregular spellings in the third person singular (él/ella/usted) and plural (ellos/ellas/ustedes) forms – e.g.:

> leer (to read) → leyó, leyeron
> caer (to fall) → cayó, cayeron

GRAMMAR

Complete the sentences using the preterite form of the verb in brackets.
1. El fin de semana pasado _____ (yo, ir) al museo.
2. Ayer _____ (nosotros, hacer) muchas cosas interesantes.
3. Ellos _____ (ver) muchos monumentos.
4. Mis padres _____ (tener) un viaje muy largo.
5. Muchos turistas _____ (venir) a mi pueblo el verano pasado.

IMPERFECT TENSE

The imperfect tense is used to describe repeated or continuous actions in the past, to describe what something or someone was like in the past, and to say what people used to do or what things used to be like – e.g. **iba** a pie todos los días (I walked every day), mi escuela primaria **era** muy pequeña (my primary school was very small), en el pasado **jugaba** al tenis (in the past I used to play tennis).

To form the imperfect you cross off the ar/er/ir endings of the infinitives and add the following endings:

	ar verbs – e.g.: jugar – to play	er verbs – e.g.: hacer – to make/do	ir verbs – e.g.: vivir – to live
yo	jugaba	hacía	vivía
tú	jugabas	hacías	vivías
él/ella/usted	jugaba	hacía	vivía
nosotros	jugábamos	hacíamos	vivíamos
vosotros	jugabais	hacíais	vivíais
ellos/ellas/ustedes	jugaban	hacían	vivían

There are three irregular verbs in the imperfect tense:

	ir – to go	ser – to be	ver – to see
yo	iba	era	veía
tú	ibas	eras	veías
él/ella/usted	iba	era	veía
nosotros	íbamos	éramos	veíamos
vosotros	ibais	erais	veíais
ellos/ellas/ustedes	iban	eran	veían

The imperfect of hay (there is/there are) is había (there was/there were). Había is a useful word for describing things in the past.

GRAMMAR

Complete the paragraph using the imperfect form of the verb in brackets.

Cuando _____ (yo, ser) más joven, _____ (nosotros, vivir) en una casa grande. Yo _____ (estar) contento porque la casa _____ (tener) un jardín enorme. Todos los días mis hermanos _____ (jugar) en el jardín.

Using the imperfect tense to describe weather

You need the imperfect tense to describe weather in the past.

Present	Imperfect
hace sol/calor etc.	hacía sol/calor etc.
está frío/nublado etc.	estaba frío/nublado etc.
nieve	nevaba
llueve	llovía

IMPERFECT CONTINUOUS TENSE

The imperfect continuous is used to say what was happening at the time of speaking. The gerund is used with the imperfect tense of the verb **estar** to form the imperfect continuous e.g. **estaba haciendo** mis deberes (I was doing my homework).

	Imperfect tense of **estar**	Gerund
yo	estaba	hablando, estudiando, escuchando, etc.
tú	estabas	
él/ella/usted	estaba	
nosotros	estábamos	
vosotros	estabais	
ellos/ellas/ustedes	estaban	

PERFECT TENSE

Use the perfect tense to say what you have done recently. It is formed with the present tense of the verb **haber** followed by the past participle. The past participle usually ends in ed in English – e.g. watched, played, visited.

To form the past participle for **ar** verbs you cross off the **ar** and add **ado**. For **er/ir** verbs, cross off the **er/ir** and add **ido** – e.g.:

estudiar (to study) ➝ estudi**ado** (studied)
comer (to eat) ➝ com**ido** (eaten)
vivir (to live) ➝ viv**ido** (lived)

	Present tense of **haber**	Past participle
yo	he	hablado, estudiado, escuchado, etc.
tú	has	
él/ella/usted	ha	
nosotros	hemos	
vosotros	habéis	
ellos/ellas/ustedes	han	

Some verbs have irregular past participles:

Infinitive	Past participle
decir – to say	dicho
escribir – to write	escrito
hacer – to make/do	hecho
poner – to put	puesto
ver – to see	visto
volver – to return	vuelto

GRAMMAR

Translate the following perfect tense sentences into English.
1. Mis amigos no han hecho sus deberes.
2. He olvidado mi cuaderno de español.
3. Hemos terminado nuestros exámenes.
4. Nunca he visitado los Estados Unidos.

PLUPERFECT TENSE

You use the pluperfect tense to say what you had done. To form the pluperfect tense you use the imperfect tense of the verb **haber** followed by the past participle.

	Imperfect tense of **haber**	Past participle
yo	había	visto, ido, estudiado, etc.
tú	habías	
él/ella/usted	había	
nosotros	habíamos	
vosotros	había	
ellos/ellas/ustedes	habían	

IMPERATIVES

Imperatives are used to give commands and instructions – e.g. ¡Haz tus deberes! (Do your homework!), ¡Siéntate! (Sit down!) The form you use depends on who you are speaking to (tú, vosotros, usted or ustedes) and if the command is positive (Stand up!) or negative (Don't stand up!).

To form positive commands using tú, just take the s off the tú form of the present tense – e.g. hablas (you speak) → ¡habla! (speak!), trabajas (you work) → ¡trabaja! (work!).

These verbs have irregular imperatives in the tú form:

decir (to say) → di
hacer (to make/do) → haz
salir (to go out) → sal
ser (to be) → sé
tener (to have) → ten

To form positive commands using vosotros, change the r at the end of the infinitive to a d – e.g. hablar → hablad, correr → corred.

You can use the third person singular (él/ella/usted) or plural (ellos/ellas/ustedes) form of the present subjunctive for formal commands – e.g. ¡tome! (take!), ¡trabaja! (work!).

You also need to use the present subjunctive form for all negative commands:

	tú	vosotros	usted	ustedes
estudi**ar**	no estudies	no estudiéis	no estudie	no estudien
beb**er**	no bebas	no bebáis	no beba	no beban
decid**ir**	no decidas	no decidáis	no decida	no decidan

PASSIVE VOICE

The passive is formed with **ser + past participle** and is used to say what is done to someone or something – e.g. mi colegio **fue construido** en los años noventa (my school was built in the nineties). You need to remember to make the past participle agree as well – e.g. mi **casa** fue **construida** el año pasado (my house was built last year).

The passive is not very common in Spanish – it is more common to avoid the passive by using the pronoun se and the third person singular (él/ella/ustedes) or plural (ellos/ellas/ustedes) form – e.g. **se recicla** el papel en el contenedor verde (paper is recycled in the green container) instead of el papel **es reciclado** en el contenedor verde, **se venden** libros en la tienda (books are sold in the shop) instead of los libros **son vendidos** en la tienda.

PRESENT SUBJUNCTIVE

The present subjunctive is a special form of a verb which is used in certain situations. You use it:

- To express doubt, uncertainty and possibility – e.g. no creo que vengan a la fiesta (I don't think they will come to the party).
- After verbs of emotion – e.g. me alegro de que mi hermana **esté** aquí (I'm glad that my sister is here).
- For wishes, advice and requests such as querer que and pedir que – e.g. mis padres quieren que **vaya** a la universidad (my parents want me to go to university).
- After para que when it means 'in order to' – e.g. mis padres me ayudan para que **saque** buenas notas (my parents help me so that/in order that I get good marks).
- After time phrases like cuando, hasta que, antes de que, etc. when you are talking about the future – e.g. cuando **termine** mis estudios (when I finish my studies).
- After the expression ojalá to say what you hope will happen – e.g. ojalá **haga** calor (let's hope it's hot).
- In certain exclamations – e.g. ¡Viva! ¡Dígame!

You form the present subjunctive by taking the final o off the yo form of the present tense and adding the present subjunctive endings:

	estudiar – to study	beber – to drink	vivir – to live
yo	estudie	beba	viva
tú	estudies	bebas	vivas
él/ella/usted	estudie	beba	viva
nosotros	estudiemos	bebamos	vivamos
vosotros	estudiéis	bebáis	viváis
ellos/ellas/ustedes	estudien	beban	vivan

Some key irregular verbs that you might see are:

	ser – to be	hacer – to make/do	ir – to go	tener – to have
yo	sea	haga	vaya	tenga
tú	seas	hagas	vayas	tengas
él/ella/usted	sea	haga	vaya	tenga
nosotros	seamos	hagamos	vayamos	tengamos
vosotros	seáis	hagáis	vayáis	tengáis
ellos/ellas/ustedes	sean	hagan	vayan	tengan

IMPERFECT SUBJUNCTIVE

One form of the imperfect subjunctive that is often used to say what you would like is quisiera. It's not as common as using me gustaría but it means the same thing.

You might use the imperfect subjunctive in si sentences (si + **imperfect subjunctive**, followed by the conditional) – e.g. **si ganara** la lotería, viajaría por todo el mundo (if I won the lottery, I would travel all over the world), **si tuviera** un trabajo, estaría muy contento (if I found a job I would be very happy).

VERB TABLES

REGULAR **AR** VERBS

Infinitive		Present	Preterite	Imperfect	Future	Conditional	Gerund/Past participle
hablar	yo	hablo	hablé	hablaba	hablaré	hablaría	hablando
— to speak	tú	hablas	hablaste	hablabas	hablarás	hablarías	hablado
	él/ella/usted	habla	habló	hablaba	hablará	hablaría	
	nosotros	hablamos	hablamos	hablábamos	hablaremos	hablaríamos	
	vosotros	habláis	hablasteis	hablabais	hablaréis	hablaríais	
	ellos/ellas/ustedes	hablan	hablaron	hablaban	hablarán	hablarían	
estudiar	yo	estudio	estudié	estudiaba	estudiaré	estudiaría	estudiando
— to study	tú	estudias	estudiaste	estudiabas	estudiarás	estudiarías	estudiado
	él/ella/usted	estudia	estudió	estudiaba	estudiará	estudiaría	
	nosotros	estudiamos	estudiamos	estudiábamos	estudiaremos	estudiaríamos	
	vosotros	estudiáis	estudiasteis	estudiabais	estudiaréis	estudiaríais	
	ellos/ellas/ustedes	estudian	estudiaron	estudiaban	estudiarán	estudiarían	

REGULAR **ER** VERBS

Infinitive		Present	Preterite	Imperfect	Future	Conditional	Gerund/Past participle
comer	yo	como	comí	comía	comeré	comería	comiendo
— to eat	tú	comes	comiste	comías	comerás	comerías	comido
	él/ella/usted	come	comió	comía	comerá	comería	
	nosotros	comemos	comimos	comíamos	comeremos	comeríamos	
	vosotros	coméis	comisteis	comíais	comeréis	comeríais	
	ellos/ellas/ustedes	comen	comieron	comían	comerán	comerían	
aprender	yo	aprendo	aprendí	aprendía	aprenderé	aprendería	aprendiendo
— to learn	tú	aprendes	aprendiste	aprendías	aprenderás	aprenderías	aprendido
	él/ella/usted	aprende	aprendió	aprendía	aprenderá	aprendería	
	nosotros	aprendemos	aprendimos	aprendíamos	aprenderemos	aprenderíamos	
	vosotros	aprendéis	aprendisteis	aprendíais	aprenderéis	aprenderíais	
	ellos/ellas/ustedes	aprenden	aprendieron	aprendían	aprenderán	aprenderían	

REGULAR **IR** VERBS

Infinitive		Present	Preterite	Imperfect	Future	Conditional	Gerund/ Past participle
vivir – to live	yo	vivo	viví	vivía	viviré	viviría	viviendo
	tú	vives	viviste	vivías	vivirás	vivirías	vivido
	él/ella/usted	vive	vivió	vivía	vivirá	viviría	
	nosotros	vivimos	vivimos	vivíamos	viviremos	viviríamos	
	vosotros	vivís	vivisteis	vivíais	viviréis	viviríais	
	ellos/ellas/ustedes	viven	vivieron	vivían	vivirán	vivirían	
recibir – to receive	yo	recibo	recibí	recibía	recibiré	recibiría	recibiendo
	tú	recibes	recibiste	recibías	recibirás	recibirías	recibido
	él/ella/usted	recibe	recibió	recibía	recibirá	recibiría	
	nosotros	recibimos	recibimos	recibíamos	recibiremos	recibiríamos	
	vosotros	recibís	recibisteis	recibíais	recibiréis	recibiríais	
	ellos/ellas/ustedes	reciben	recibieron	recibían	recibirán	recibirían	

LIST OF COMMON REGULAR VERBS

Common regular ar verbs

abandonar – to abandon/leave/give up

acabar – to complete/finish/end

acampar – to camp/go camping

aceptar – to accept

acompañar – to accompany/go along

aconsejar – to counsel/advise

acostumbrar – to be accustomed/be in the habit of

adaptar – to adapt

admirar – to admire

adoptar – to adopt

adorar – to adore/worship

ahorrar – to save

alimentar – to feed/nourish/sustain

alquilar – to rent/hire

alterar – to alter/change/disturb/upset

amar – to love

anunciar – to announce

apoyar – to support/lean against

ayudar – to help/assist/aid

bailar – to dance

bajar – to lower/go down/download

bañarse – to have a bath/a swim

besar – to kiss

brindar – to toast/offer

cambiar – to change

caminar – to walk

cancelar – to cancel

cansarse – to tire out/get tired

cantar – to sing

casarse – to marry/get married

causar – to cause/bring about/create

celebrar – to celebrate

cenar – to eat dinner/supper

charlar – to chat/talk

cocinar – to cook

combinar – to combine

comentar – to comment

comparar – to compare

completar – to complete

comprar – to buy

concentrar – to concentrate

conectar – to connect

confirmar – to confirm

conservar – to conserve/save/preserve

considerar – to consider

contaminar – to contaminate

contestar – to answer/respond/reply

controlar – to control

cortar – to cut

crear – to create

cuidar – to take care of

curar – to cure/heal

decorar – to decorate

dejar – to leave/let/leave alone/let stand

desarrollar – to develop

desayunar – to eat breakfast

descansar – to rest

desear – to wish/desire

desenchufar – to unplug

desengañar – to disillusion/disabuse

dibujar – to draw

disfrutar – to enjoy/take enjoyment in

ducharse – to have a shower

emborracharse – to get drunk

empeorar – to worsen/make worse/deteriorate

emplear – to employ/use/hire

enamorarse – to fall in love

enseñar – to show/teach

entrar – to enter/go in

entrevistar – to interview

escapar – to escape

escuchar – to listen/hear

esperar – to wait/hope

estornudar – to sneeze

estudiar – to study

evitar – to avoid

faltar – to lack/miss/be missing

fumar – to smoke

ganar – to win/earn/gain

gastar – to spend (money)

grabar – to record

gritar – to scream/shout/yell

hablar – to speak/talk

ingresar – to enter/join a group/become a member

iniciar – to initiate/start

intentar – to intend/try

invitar – to invite

irritar – to irritate

lavar(se) – to wash (oneself)

levantar(se) – to lift/get (oneself) up

limitar – to limit

limpiar – to clean/wipe

llamar – to call

llenar – to fill/make full

llevar – to take (literally)/wear/carry

llorar – to cry

luchar – to fight/battle/wage war

madurar – to mature/ripen

mandar – to send/order/command

mejorar – to make better/get better/improve

mencionar – to mention

mirar – to watch/see/look

nadar – to swim

necesitar – to need

notar – to note

observar – to observe

odiar – to hate

olvidar – to forget

parar – to stop

participar – to participate

pasar – to pass/spend (time)

preguntar – to ask (a question)

preocupar(se) – to worry/preoccupy/concern (oneself)

preparar – to prepare/fix/get ready

presentar – to present

prestar – to lend/let borrow/loan

programar – to program

quedar – to stay/remain

quejarse – to complain

quemar(se) – to burn (oneself)

quitar – to remove/take off/take away

regresar – to return/go back/give back

reparar – to repair/fix

respetar – to respect

saludar – to greet/say hello

salvar – to save

señalar – to wave/signal/point out/indicate

terminar – to terminate/end/finish/stop

tirar – to throw/pull

tolerar – to tolerate/put up with/endure

tomar – to drink/take (figuratively)

trabajar – to work

trasladar – to move/transfer

tratar – to treat/try

usar – to use

viajar – to travel/take a trip

visitar – to visit

Common regular er verbs

aprender – to learn

beber – to drink

comer – to eat

cometer – to commit

comprender – to comprehend/understand

correr – to run

deber – to owe/ought to

depender – to depend

esconder – to hide

meter – to insert/put in

proceder – to proceed

prometer – to promise

responder – to reply/respond

Common regular ir verbs

abrir – to open

admitir – to admit/permit

añadir – to add

asistir – to attend (e.g. classes)

compartir – to share

cubrir – to cover/put the lid on

cumplir – to complete/finish/reach (an age)

decidir – to decide

describir – to describe

descubrir – to discover/uncover

discutir – to discuss

distinguir – to distinguish

dividir – to divide

escribir – to write (but note this has an irregular past participle)

imprimir – to print

ocurrir – to occur/happen

partir – to divide/leave

permitir – to permit/allow/let

prohibir – to prohibit/forbid/ban

recibir – to receive

subir – to rise/climb/go up/board

sufrir – to suffer/endure

vivir – to live/be alive

IRREGULAR VERB TABLES

Infinitive		Present	Preterite	Imperfect	Future	Conditional	Gerund/ Past participle
dar — to give	yo	doy	di	daba	daré	daría	dando
	tú	das	diste	dabas	darás	darías	dado
	él/ella/usted	da	dio	daba	dará	daría	
	nosotros	damos	dimos	dábamos	daremos	daríamos	
	vosotros	dais	disteis	dabais	daréis	daríais	
	ellos/ellas/ustedes	dan	dieron	daban	darán	darían	
decir — to say	yo	digo	dije	decía	diré	diría	diciendo
	tú	dices	dijiste	decías	dirás	dirías	dicho
	él/ella/usted	dice	dijo	decía	dirá	diría	
	nosotros	decimos	dijimos	decíamos	diremos	diríamos	
	vosotros	decís	dijisteis	decíais	diréis	diríais	
	ellos/ellas/ustedes	dicen	dijeron	decían	dirán	dirían	
estar — to be	yo	estoy	estuve	estaba	estaré	estaría	estando
	tú	estás	estuviste	estabas	estarás	estarías	estado
	él/ella/usted	está	estuvo	estaba	estará	estaría	
	nosotros	estamos	estuvimos	estábamos	estaremos	estaríamos	
	vosotros	estáis	estuvisteis	estabais	estaréis	estaríais	
	ellos/ellas/ustedes	están	estuvieron	estaban	estarán	estarían	
haber — to have	yo	he	hube	había	habré	habría	habiendo
	tú	has	hubiste	habías	habrás	habrías	habido
	él/ella/usted	ha	hubo	había	habrá	habría	
	nosotros	hemos	hubimos	habíamos	habremos	habríamos	
	vosotros	habéis	hubisteis	habíais	habréis	habríais	
	ellos/ellas/ustedes	han	hubieron	habían	habrán	habrían	
hacer — to make/do	yo	hago	hice	hacía	haré	haría	haciendo
	tú	haces	hiciste	hacías	harás	harías	hecho
	él/ella/usted	hace	hizo	hacía	hará	haría	
	nosotros	hacemos	hicimos	hacíamos	haremos	haríamos	
	vosotros	hacéis	hicisteis	hacíais	haréis	haríais	
	ellos/ellas/ustedes	hacen	hicieron	hacían	harán	harían	

Infinitive		Present	Preterite	Imperfect	Future	Conditional	Gerund/Past participle
ir — to go	yo	voy	fui	iba	iré	iría	yendo
	tú	vas	fuiste	ibas	irás	irías	ido
	él/ella/usted	va	fue	iba	irá	iría	
	nosotros	vamos	fuimos	íbamos	iremos	iríamos	
	vosotros	vais	fuisteis	ibais	iréis	iríais	
	ellos/ellas/ustedes	van	fueron	iban	irán	irían	
poder — to be able to	yo	puedo	pude	podía	podré	podría	pudiendo
	tú	puedes	pudiste	podías	podrás	podrías	podido
	él/ella/usted	puede	pudo	podía	podrá	podría	
	nosotros	podemos	pudimos	podíamos	podremos	podríamos	
	vosotros	podéis	pudisteis	podíais	podréis	podríais	
	ellos/ellas/ustedes	pueden	pudieron	podían	podrán	podrían	
poner — to put	yo	pongo	puse	ponía	pondré	pondría	poniendo
	tú	pones	pusiste	ponías	pondrás	pondrías	puesto
	él/ella/usted	pone	puso	ponía	pondrá	pondría	
	nosotros	ponemos	pusimos	poníamos	pondremos	pondríamos	
	vosotros	ponéis	pusisteis	poníais	pondréis	pondríais	
	ellos/ellas/ustedes	ponen	pusieron	ponían	pondrán	pondrían	
querer — to want	yo	quiero	quise	quería	querré	querría	queriendo
	tú	quieres	quisiste	querías	querrás	querrías	querido
	él/ella/usted	quiere	quiso	quería	querrá	querría	
	nosotros	queremos	quisimos	queríamos	querremos	querríamos	
	vosotros	queréis	quisisteis	queríais	querréis	querríais	
	ellos/ellas/ustedes	quieren	quisieron	querían	querrán	querrían	
saber — to know	yo	sé	supe	sabía	sabré	sabría	sabiendo
	tú	sabes	supiste	sabías	sabrás	sabrías	sabido
	él/ella/usted	sabe	supo	sabía	sabrá	sabría	
	nosotros	sabemos	supimos	sabíamos	sabremos	sabríamos	
	vosotros	sabéis	supisteis	sabíais	sabréis	sabríais	
	ellos/ellas/ustedes	saben	supieron	sabían	sabrán	sabrían	

Infinitive		Present	Preterite	Imperfect	Future	Conditional	Gerund/Past participle
salir – to go out	yo	salgo	salí	salía	saldré	saldría	saliendo salido
	tú	sales	saliste	salías	saldrás	saldrías	
	él/ella/usted	sale	salió	salía	saldrá	saldría	
	nosotros	salimos	salimos	salíamos	saldremos	saldríamos	
	vosotros	salís	salisteis	salíais	saldréis	saldríais	
	ellos/ellas/ustedes	saben	salieron	salían	saldrán	saldrían	
ser – to be	yo	soy	fui	era	seré	sería	siendo sido
	tú	eres	fuiste	eras	serás	serías	
	él/ella/usted	es	fue	era	será	sería	
	nosotros	somos	fuimos	éramos	seremos	seríamos	
	vosotros	sois	fuisteis	erais	seréis	seríais	
	ellos/ellas/ustedes	son	fueron	eran	serán	serían	
tener – to have	yo	tengo	tuve	tenía	tendré	tendría	teniendo tenido
	tú	tienes	tuviste	tenías	tendrá	tendrías	
	él/ella/usted	tiene	tuvo	tenía	tendrás	tendría	
	nosotros	tenemos	tuvimos	teníamos	tendremos	tendríamos	
	vosotros	tenéis	tuvisteis	teníais	tendréis	tendríais	
	ellos/ellas/ustedes	tienen	tuvieron	tenían	tendrán	tendrían	
venir – to come	yo	vengo	vine	venía	vendré	vendría	viniendo venido
	tú	vienes	viniste	venías	vendrás	vendrías	
	él/ella/usted	viene	vino	venía	vendrá	vendría	
	nosotros	venimos	vinimos	veníamos	vendremos	vendríamos	
	vosotros	venís	vinisteis	veníais	vendréis	vendríais	
	ellos/ellas/ustedes	vienen	vinieron	venían	vendrán	vendrían	
ver – to see	yo	veo	vi	veía	veré	vería	viendo visto
	tú	ves	viste	veías	verás	verías	
	él/ella/usted	ve	vio	veía	verá	vería	
	nosotros	vemos	vimos	veíamos	veremos	veríamos	
	vosotros	veis	visteis	veíais	veréis	veríais	
	ellos/ellas/ustedes	ven	vieron	veían	verán	verían	

ANSWERS

SELF AND RELATIONSHIPS

Page 21

1. My aunt is hard-working, sporty and very intelligent.
2. When I was younger, I used to have/I had lots of friends.
3. Unfortunately, my best friend doesn't get on well with his parents.
4. What are the most important personal qualities of a good friend?

TECHNOLOGY AND SOCIAL MEDIA

Page 25

1. Addicted to social media.
2. Up to three hours a day.
3. 18%
4. b

HEALTH AND FITNESS

Page 31

1. A gym/personal training/fitness plans.
2. Design a personalised fitness plan/monitor your diet/propose a nutritional plan (**any two**).
3. Training with a partner/a training session for two people.
4. It's for the month of February/you can get five sessions for 65 euros.
5. Their website/follow them on social media (**any one**).

ENTERTAINMENT AND LEISURE

Page 35

1. Raquel
2. Lara
3. Arturo
4. Arturo
5. Lara
6. Raquel

Page 37

1. La semana pasada fui de compras y gasté mucho dinero.
2. El fin de semana que viene voy a ir al cine con mi familia.
3. ¿Qué te gusta hacer en tu tiempo libre?
4. No puedo salir mañana porque tengo demasiados deberes.

FOOD AND DRINK

Page 41

1. In the entrance of the restaurant.
2. Cookery books.
3. They were boring/he wasn't interested in them.
4. It had pretty pictures.
5. It was first time in his life that he had read a recipe book.

FESTIVALS AND CELEBRATIONS

Page 45

The music festival took place last weekend. My parents let me go with my friends for the first time. Many tourists came to the village for the event and I had a great time. I love camping and listening to live music and I want to return to the same festival next year. It's going to be incredible!

LOCAL AREAS OF INTEREST

Page 51

1. c
2. f
3. a
4. d

Page 53

Me gusta vivir en mi ciudad porque hay muchas cosas que hacer para los jóvenes. En el pasado no había un cine, pero ahora hay un centro comercial grande cerca del rio. En mi opinión, necesitamos/nos hacen falta más autobuses. En el futuro, me gustaría vivir en España porque me encanta la cultura española y hace sol.

TRANSPORT

Page 55

1. Watching TV.
2. There had been a car crash/two cars had collided.
3. They bought it together last year.
4. She opened the door (of the car) and helped him to get out.

LOCAL AND REGIONAL FEATURES AND CHARACTERISTICS

Page 61

The castle is a very popular tourist destination and it is located in the city centre to the right of the park. It is open every day from ten o'clock and entry is free on Sundays and bank holidays. I went to the monument yesterday and it was very educational. For me, it is very important to discover the culture and history of a region. Tomorrow I would like to visit the museum.

HOLIDAYS AND TOURISM

Page 65

Rita: c
Miguel: d
Xavi: f
Marina: a

Page 67

Normalmente **voy** de vacaciones con mis padres y **nos quedamos** en un camping. Lo **paso** bastante bien, pero este verano **iré** a Francia con mis amigos. **Viajaremos** en barco y **nos quedaremos** en un albergue. El año pasado **fui** a Alemania con mi colegio. **Hicimos** muchas cosas divertidas y **visitamos** muchos sitios de interés. En general **prefiero** las vacaciones activas porque **soy** una persona deportista.

ENVIRONMENT

Page 71

to help
to protect
to respect
to save
to improve
to recycle
to pollute
to clean

to destroy
to damage

Page 71

1. Iván
2. Antonio
3. Lena
4. Oli
5. Ismael
6. Zaca

SOCIAL ISSUES

Page 75

1. Promote/defend children's rights.
2. Contributions/donations (from citizens and from the private sector).
3. They are fundamental for saving lives and protecting children.
4. Send money immediately to help in an emergency/humanitarian crisis.
5. Online or by bank transfer.

SCHOOL/COLLEGE LIFE

Page 81

1. If they weren't paying attention.
2. At breaktime/when the bell rings for break.
3. The rules are different/there is a rule that any item taken from pupils by teachers during class time goes to room '15/60'.
4. On the ground floor/next to the staffroom.
5. They give the item to the head teacher and, at the end of the day, he takes it to the room.

SCHOOL/COLLEGE STUDIES

Page 85

1. It will help you to improve your career/speak to people from other countries/enjoy your holidays more (**any two**).
2. They are happier and richer.
3. Learning more languages.
4. Helps people understand that the world isn't all the same/that there is cultural diversity/prepares them for the future.

WORK EXPERIENCE AND PART-TIME JOBS

Page 91

1. b

2. c
3. a
4. c

SKILLS AND PERSONAL QUALITIES
Page 95
1. d
2. g
3. i
4. j
5. b
6. f
7. a
8. h
9. c
10. e

APPLYING FOR WORK/STUDY
Page 101
1. I don't intend to go to university, because it's too expensive.
2. I'm going to leave school after my exams because I would prefer to earn lots of money.
3. I had an interview yesterday afternoon and I was quite nervous.
4. I'm prepared/ready to study hard and I hope to get very good grades.
5. Business has always interested me and my objective is to work in a big company.

CAREER PLANS
Page 105
1. Leadership/global vision (**any one**).
2. Two years.
3. Personalised support/a personal mentor/ connections with more than 2,700 firms (**any two**).
4. The quality of the teachers/the use of technology in classes/the international focus on campus/the improvement in your level of English/the chance to go on international exchanges (**any three**).

Page 107
Quiero viajar a muchos lugares después de la universidad. A corto plazo, me gustaría pasar un año sabático en el extranjero. Espero trabajar en una organización internacional y aprender sobre distintas culturas. Sería una experiencia inolvidable. Cuando era

más joven/pequeño/a, siempre tenía ganas de/quería aprender un nuevo idioma/una nueva lengua.

GRAMMAR
Page 114
1. For me, the most important thing is helping other people.
2. I think that the worst problem is immigration.
3. In my opinion, poverty is more serious than conflict.
4. Immigration is as serious as terrorism.
5. I think that the most urgent situation is the economic crisis.
6. It is easier to sell cakes than ask for donations.

Page 116
1. tranquilamente
2. rápidamente
3. activamente
4. frecuentemente
5. malsanamente

Page 124
1. I have been playing tennis for six months.
2. I have been a vegetarian for three years.
3. Jorge has been playing basketball since he was small/young.
4. I have been living here since I was born.

Page 125
1. Mi hermano **vive** con su novia.
2. Mis amigos **hablan** demasiado.
3. Cada noche yo **chateo** en Internet.
4. Mi familia y yo siempre **cenamos** juntos.
5. Yo **creo** que la amistad es importante.
6. Los jóvenes **utilizan** la tecnología todo el tiempo.

Page 128
1. Mi hermana **prefiere** salir con sus amigos.
2. Irma no **tiene** muchos deberes.
3. Mis tíos **quieren** separarse.
4. Nosotros **podemos** salir hasta muy tarde.
5. Mis padres **son** muy estrictos.

Page 129
1. Cada persona **es** diferente.
2. Algunos padres **están** preocupados por sus hijos.

3. Mi hermana **es** alta y guapa.
4. Prefiero **estar** con mis amigos.
5. Es aburrido (it is boring – all the time). Estoy aburrida (I am bored – at the moment).
6. Marina es bonita (Marina is pretty – she is always pretty). Marina está bonita (Marina looks pretty – at the moment).

Page 131
1. Voy a tener hijos.
2. Vamos a vivir en una casa grande.
3. Mis amigos van a escribir un blog.
4. Mi hermana va a salir con su novio.

Page 132
1. I will live in a flat with my friends.
2. Tomorrow I will buy a new mobile phone.
3. Technology will be more important in the future.
4. My parents will not be very happy.

Page 132
1. En el futuro **me gustaría** estudiar el español.
2. **Sacaría** buenas notas en mis exámenes.
3. Mi profesor ideal **sería** divertido.
4. Mi colegio ideal **tendría** instalaciones modernas.
5. **Estudiaría** en la universidad.
6. Mis amigos **irían** al club de baloncesto.

Page 133
1. La semana pasada nosotros **visitamos** los monumentos.
2. Ayer **viajé** al colegio en coche.
3. Mis padres **compraron** un billete.
4. Ayer **salí** con mis amigos.
5. ¿Cómo **viajaste** de vacaciones el año pasado?

Page 134
1. El fin de semana pasado **fui** al museo.
2. Ayer **hicimos** muchas cosas interesantes.
3. Ellos **vieron** muchos monumentos.
4. Mis padres **tuvieron** un viaje muy largo.
5. Muchos turistas **vinieron** a mi pueblo el verano pasado.

Page 135
Cuando **era** más joven, **vivíamos** en una casa grande. Yo **estaba** contento porque la casa **tenía** un jardín enorme. Todos los días mis hermanos **jugaban** en el jardín.

Page 137
1. My friends have not done their homework.
2. I have forgotten my Spanish book.
3. We have finished our exams.
4. I have never visited the United States.